for Retirement Is Not for Sissies

HAROLD MYRA
long-time Executive Chair and CEO
of Christianity Today International, recently retired

David gives us a personal tour through the realities of retirement, supplying lots of stories and illustrations. An accessible, realistic guide with plenty of breadth.

VERNON GROUNDS
retired Denver Seminary Chancellor

Retirement Is Not for Sissies embodies the wisdom, the insight, and the humor I anticipate whenever I begin to read anything McKenna writes. Some topics obviously don't lend themselves to any facetious touch, but this collection of sage observations and most helpful counsel calls for the kind of delightful treatment he has given it. I hope it gains the appreciative readership it deserves.

KAREN O'CONNOR
author, *Gettin' Old Ain't for Wimps* (Harvest House, 2004), *Walkin' with God Ain't for Wimps* (Harvest House, 2007), *The Golden Years Ain't for Wimps* (Harvest House, 2008)

Want to make your retirement count for even more than your years at the office? David McKenna's book *Retirement Is Not For Sissies* will help you become informed and inspired to finish strong and well. The author's six key steps for achieving this goal are wrapped in real-life anecdotes, bits of humor, and plenty of sound wisdom. A must-read for any retiree and anyone within retirement's reach.

ALVIN O. AUSTIN
Chancellor and President Emeritus, LeTourneau University

David McKenna is an artist with words and this may be his best-ever book. As one who just stepped into the world of retirement, I found this book to be a masterpiece of insight, humor, practical and personal advice, and spiritual challenge that hit the target for me. If you are thinking about retirement or have already made the plunge, you will want to read *Retirement Is Not for Sissies*.

FRANK HAAS
General Partner, Leisure Communities, Ltd.

This book mirrors many of the stories I have heard from thousands of new retirees in our active adult communities. I would have given it as a house-warming gift to our newly retired residents if it had been available earlier; it would have had a great positive impact on their "new" life. I, personally, have changed from scheduled responsibilities (work) to chosen activities and responsibilities (retired, why don't I like that word?) and I find Dave's book to be very relevant for me. This is an excellent book for those soon to enter or already in the "golden years."

PAUL K. KLEIN
retired Director, U.S. West;
retired Vice President, Telephone Pioneers of America

A must-read for anyone feeling the effects of aging, and for people about to retire. More useful than a company gold watch stored in a drawer. Many great insights into the challenges, changes, and nuances retirement life offers. Guaranteed to improve motivation and planning, enhance outlook and purpose, and help its readers find "success." Good humorous illustrations. Provides a wonderful, balanced look into both physical and spiritual needs during aging and this finite earthly life.

DAVID O. MOBERG
Professor Emeritus, Marquette University;
editor, *Aging and Spirituality* (Haworth Press, 2001)

This "survival kit" is a delight to read. Packed with upbeat wisdom that's confirmed by fascinating personal experiences, it shares reflections and insights about aging as it *really* is. Its 30 short chapters can be read in any order for sheer enjoyment or for sage advice before or during retirement. They suggest how and how not to deal with unanticipated incidents, puzzling demands, and trying circumstances related to relationships, class reunions, marriage, residences, personal identity, age discrimination, sex, leisure, humor, exercise, health, memory, possessions, economic adjustments, investments, politics, spirituality, and countless other concerns of the final third of life.

NANCY AND NORM EDWARDS
retired executive team, Counsel in Resource Development

Out of his own experiences, David McKenna addresses nearly every issue the retiree or soon-to-be retiree will face. With practical and sometimes humorous insights, we realize we have a lot of company. As we shared our reading, we asked ourselves, "How did Dave know that about us?" He helps us realize that the best days are yet to come.

GEORGE DUFF
former President, Greater Seattle Chamber of Commerce

David McKenna has written an extremely practical book for those who are approaching the end of their primary career or even those who have moved on to the next "act." The scriptural admonition to redeem the time is even more important. As we think about passing the baton—and as long as we are in the race we should still have a baton—we must simplify, as Dave suggests, so that those we care about and those who care about us will have a smooth transition.

GEORGE K. BRUSHABER
retired President, Bethel University (St. Paul, Minnesota)

What a "just in time" gift David McKenna has given me. As I write this I am within days of completing a four-decade career of leadership in Christian higher education, and everyone has proposed a plan for the rest of my life. But armed with McKenna's wisdom and counsel, my wife and I embark on a new life journey with hope and confidence. Thank you, David, for once again mentoring me.

BRUCE DINGMAN
President, The Dingman Company

Perhaps the best book on "redeployment" ever written. A great "how-to" for the soon-to-be or recently retired Christian.

GLENN E. WHITE
retired Chrysler Corporation Vice President

McKenna's book supports the old statement, "Whoever said 'These are the golden years' was probably not yet retired." Yet *Retirement Is Not for Sissies* is full of good ideas and thought on how to take the lemons that retirement can throw at you and turn them into lemonade. McKenna also reminds us all that Christians in retirement continue to live in a mission field and we have responsibility as to how we live and interact with others. The book has lots of good stories folded in with advice and counsel that can help make retirement an enjoyable and worthwhile time of life.

GERALD E. BATES
Bishop Emeritus, Free Methodist Church of North America

Retirement Is Not for Sissies is experienced, insightful, reflective, and full of humor. For retirees and those about to be retired, David McKenna's book is a priceless road map into hope.

Retirement Is Not for Sissies

a game plan for seniors

David L. McKenna

BARCLAY PRESS

Newberg, Oregon

RETIREMENT IS NOT FOR SISSIES
A Game Plan for Seniors

© 2008 by David L. McKenna

Published by Barclay Press
211 N. Meridian St., #101, Newberg, OR 97132
www.barclaypress.com

ISBN 978-1-59498-014-5

All Scripture quotations, unless otherwise indicated, are taken from the *Holy Bible, New International Version®. NIV®.* Copyright © 1973, 1978, 1984 by International Bible Society. Used by permission of Zondervan. All rights reserved.

Scripture verses marked KJV are from the King James Version of the Bible.

DEDICATED TO

My Retired Classmates
50 years and counting

Ypsilanti High School, Class of '47

Spring Arbor Junior College, Class of '49

Western Michigan University, Class of '51

Asbury Theological Seminary, Class of '53

University of Michigan, Class of '55 & '58

Contents

Part III—Think Young

Part IV—Laugh At Yourself

Part V—Grow Down

Part VI—Lean Forward

Epilogue

An Agenda
for Aging

Millions of believers are joining the swelling ranks of people retiring earlier and living longer. With this epic change comes the unprecedented opportunity to witness to our faith in new spheres of spirit and character. God calls us to live in love and serve with joy, in sharp contrast to the pursuit of pleasure and the hope of happiness based upon mere self-interest.

So as a start toward that future from one who is already there, in the following pages I offer the following survival tools for Christian retirees of all ages:

- Accept reality
- Expect surprises
- Think young
- Laugh at yourself
- Grow down
- Lean forward

Fourteen years ago, at the age of sixty-five, I resigned from the presidency of Asbury Theological Seminary to test the waters of retirement. That is when the real fun began.

Every day had its surprise. Even though I relished my freedom from a daily schedule and the resulting release of creative energy to write a book a year, I discovered things about myself, my work, my relationships, and my faith that are unique to the retirement setting. I expect that you are making some of the same discoveries.

Then, as age crept up and I made a turn into the seventies, more surprises lay in store. Although I did some serious learning, more often than not, the incidents that provoked the lessons were funny, and sometimes hilarious. So as I began to jot down notes about my experiences, I found that humorous questions set the stage for more serious discussion.

Jesus gives us the example when he tells the ludicrous story about the camel squeezing through the eye of the needle. Biblical scholars who try to find some rational explanation for the story miss the point. Jesus is using humor as a powerful teaching tool. His story might well be introduced by a riddle, "How does a camel go through the eye of a needle?" Our four-year-old grandson will laugh out loud at the question and then ask with wide eyes, "How, Grandpa?" I ask my readers to adopt the same childlike curiosity when they see the titles to the chapters that follow and read to find out what the question means.

"Enjoy Life. You Won't Get Out of It Alive." There is truth in this bumper sticker, especially when we retire and as we age. It may be the motto for a hedonist, but it also has something important to say to those of us who take life so seriously that we miss the fun of learning the lessons that God has planned for us in our retirement.

All retirees, young or old, need meaning in their lives in addition to fun. In other words, we must retire *to* something as well as *from* something. In *Retirement Is Not For Sissies*, I share that a whole new world awaits us as we live in love, grow in grace, and serve with joy while enjoying our newfound freedom.

PART I

Accept Reality

Who's a Sissy?

Bette Davis, the legendary movie star, put a bundle of truth in a nutshell when she said, "Old age is not for sissies." As an aging woman whose prior success depended upon youthful beauty, she struck a somber note of truth. While most of us do not have her problem of fading glamour, we know what she means by the challenges of old age.

With advancing years come the grim realities of declining energy, health, and memory. Even people of great faith and a growing spirit will agree that old age puts to test our grit and our grace.

Old age can kill you.

Retirement is the new kid on the block in the aging process. Less than a century ago, retirement was almost unknown. Our society was divided between the leisure classes and the working masses. Members of the leisure class either made or inherited fortunes that permitted them to work or play at an age of their choice. People of the working class, especially in a farm economy, did not have this option. As partners in extended families, they continued to work until the day they died.

But when the factory replaced the farm and the city replaced the village, everything changed. Urban workers on the assembly line burned out early and lacked a support system for old age. Presto! As the centerpiece for the welfare state, Social Security—with a mandatory retirement age—became the answer.

Make no mistake. Retirement is here to stay. It is part and parcel of our culture. The ranks of aging retirees swell every year, while the entry age of retirees is falling rapidly. At issue are some of the highest priorities for our nation—the cost of quality health care, the viability of Social Security, the stability of pension funds, the impact of inheritance and tax policies, the needs of the new poor among the elderly, and the political implications of the fastest growing cohort among all age groups. Hand in hand, retirement and aging are taking us into an uncertain future.

Christians are not exempt from the social, financial, and political consequences of retirement and aging. We are one with our neighbors in our responsibility for dealing with these issues. More than that, the body of Christ has an unprecedented opportunity to minister on the growing edge of the changing dynamics represented by retirement and aging. The least, the lost, the littlest, and the loneliest among us can be found among early retirees as a well as elderly seniors. Long before the full impact of a retired and aging population reaches the top of our evangelical agenda, individual members of the body of Christ have the opportunity to model the ministry of meaningful, contented, and joyful living.

Sissies need not apply.

2

Can Billy Graham Be Wrong?

When our oldest son, Douglas, dared—in his doctoral research—to challenge the theory of a renowned psychologist, his advisor warned him, "If you fight a giant, you had better kill him with the first stone."

I feel the same way when I dare to ask the question, "Can Billy Graham be wrong?" In my mind, he is a giant for everything that is right. To suggest that he is wrong is like David slinging the first stone. I had better be right on target!

While under no circumstances do I want to destroy him, I do have one smooth stone of difference regarding the question of retirement. Knowing that Graham has a sense of humor, I can imagine him urging me, "Sling it, David. I could be wrong."

Is Retirement Biblical?

Graham and I do not disagree on many things. Retirement is the exception. In response to the question, "Can a Christian retire?" Graham said, "I don't see anybody in Scripture retiring from preaching.[1]" Graham preached until he was 86 years old, nearly blind, and barely able to stand.

Graham's response awakens guilt in me. We all have some sayings etched into our childhood memories that continue to shape us. Graham's comment that he finds no biblical basis for retirement takes me back to my childhood and a camp meeting evangelist who hammered into my head: "I would rather burn out than rust out." For him choosing to retire was not an option. Graham, who held the same belief, only retired when his health prevented him from continuing to preach.

While respecting Graham's viewpoint and admiring his decision, I have to ask: What about the millions of us who *are* retired, either by a voluntary decision or mandatory action? Can we reconcile retirement with our Christian commitment?

It is true that the Bible does not specifically speak to the subject of retirement. Yet neither does it address stem cell research, health care, homosexual marriage, or gun control. As with so many modern issues, we have to count on the spirit of the Word rather than the letter of the law to guide us.

Time on Our Hands

Retirement is a biblical issue because it deals with the stewardship of time. Jesus gave an almost equal amount of attention to talking about our responsibility for our use of time as he did to talking about money. Retirement, therefore, is a major issue for Christians because of one indisputable fact: We are retiring earlier and living longer.

Let me use a personal example. In the 1930s when the retirement age of sixty-five was enacted, the average life span for a man was seventy years. Social Security payments were computed on the assumption that the average male would live for five years after retirement. When my father retired in the 1960s at the mandatory age of sixty-five, he had worked forty-five years—but his life expectancy had risen to seventy-three. Thirty years later, when I voluntarily retired at the age of sixty-five, I had worked for forty years and had a life expectancy of eighty-three.

Seven years after my retirement, in 2002, our oldest son chose early retirement at the age of fifty. He had worked for twenty-five years and has a life expectancy of eighty-eight.

While actuarial tables projected eight years of retirement for my father, I am scheduled for eighteen, and our son is on track for thirty-three years as a retiree. The balance has tipped. Our son will spend more time in retirement than in career!

Our family history is not the exception. We mirror the trends of a society in which more people are retiring earlier and living longer. Soon, the ranks of retirees will become a dominant cohort in the general population and a powerful influence in the Christian community. We cannot ignore this fact without defaulting on our opportunity to make retirement a meaningful witness to our faith. Our responsibility is clear. On a sound biblical basis, we must build a retirement ethic that balances our work ethic.

The Secular Bluff

Try as we might, we cannot wish away the question, "Can Christians retire?" Unless we have an answer based upon biblical principles, we will get sucked into the vortex of what can be called the "secular bluff."

Because the term *secular* has become almost inseparably joined with *humanism*, we may miss the root meaning of the word. *Secular* simply means "time-oriented." Rather than taking a spiritual or eternal view of time, a secularist limits time to the present moment and the pleasure of that moment. And here is another instance where Christians are victims of a vacuum.

The secular bluff, applied to retirement, tells us that our time belongs to *us*, without discipline or accountability. The fallout is obvious. In retirement, The secular bluff tells us that we earn the right of self-interest, free ourselves for pleasure, deserve the bliss of happiness, and escape from our responsibility to God. In its extreme form, the secular bluff reinforces the radical individualism against which Robert Bellah warned in his book *Habits of the Heart*. We dare say, "I will be what I want to be for my own happiness" or "I will do what I want to do for my own pleasure."[2]

We desperately need biblical correctives to contest the arrogance of our secular society and its postmodern mind. Of all people, senior citizens should exemplify a mindset that sees life in the perspective of eternity and believes in the reality of the supernatural. Long ago, we seniors should have learned that there is *no* personal happiness without spiritual peace.

The Issue Is Stewardship

I believe that the Bible addresses the question of retirement when Jesus talks about our responsibility for the resources of time and money that he gives us. Stewardship, a favorite subject of Jesus, immediately checks into our thinking.

Retirees are persons with time on their hands, money in their pocket, and experience in their portfolio. These are the resources upon which stewardship is built. So while the Bible may not speak specifically about retirement, it gives top attention to several principles upon which Christian stewardship is built.

In retirement, we must relearn the lesson of the faithful steward: *We are the owners of nothing, managers of everything, and accountable to God for all.* Rather than assuming we are the owners of happiness, the managers of selective morality, and the accountants to our own interest, we find ourselves humbled in the servant's role.

We do not need the Bible to speak specifically about the meaning of modern retirement, for the principle is clear. In response to the question "Can Christians retire?" we have an answer: *Christians can retire from career, but never from ministry.*

Knowing Billy Graham as I do, I am quite sure that he will be quick to agree. But let's look deeper into what this means. Let's change the question from "Can Christians retire?" to "Is retirement a ministry?"

PART **II**

Expect Surprises

3

Where Is Everyone Going on Monday Morning?

Retirement is a succession of shocks. The first shock is to awaken on Monday morning and wonder where everyone is going.

Our knee-jerk reaction is to get up and go with them. After all, habits of a lifetime do not get wiped out by a retirement party or a gold watch. In fact, psychologists tell us that habits that persist become driving motivations.

"Wait," you say. "Who would ever miss the gridlock during the rush hour that doubles the commute time? What is the fun of sipping coffee, listening to talk radio, talking on a cell phone, or reading a book, while inching along both morning and night?"

How many times have we said that the best thing about retirement is the freedom from the steering wheel? Haven't we read the statistics that show 80 percent of Americans hate to get up and go to work on Monday morning?

Perhaps. But why, then, do we feel a twinge on Monday morning in the early stages of our retirement? Is it a pinch of guilt about not going to work? Is it a bit of nostalgia for past days? Or is it a slight admission that we miss the pain? At the risk of giving a simple answer to a complex question, let me try to offer an explanation.

The Old Work Ethic

Retirees sixty-five years of age or older are Geezers born during The Great Depression. This includes me.

Although I have given up telling the story to my grandchildren, the fact is that I hit the stage in the same year that Al Jolson made "Sonny Boy" famous. That explains why I was called "Sonny Boy" for the first four years of my life. I am dated.

Another bit of personal history: I distinctly remember my fifth birthday. We'd lived on welfare for months, but my father had recently secured a job loading rail cars for the Ford Motor Company. He had no money to buy me a birthday present, but brought home a black rubber washer with a hole in the middle (it was used to cushion the engines shipped on the rail cars). Dad hid the washer in his lunch pail and teased me into finding my "birthday present." After I dug it out from the bottom of the pail, I held it up and silently shrugged the question, *What is it?*

"When winter comes," Dad said, "it will make a good hockey puck."

He was right. With the first freeze of the pond in the park, my puck and I became the envy of the neighborhood.

Poverty has its own creativity.

I started work at the age of nine, delivering *The Saturday Evening Post*, *The Country Gentleman*, and *Lady's Home Journal* to a weekly route of customers. Three years later, I biked across town every afternoon to deliver *The Ypsilanti Daily Press* to 125 homes in a span of two hours. In quick order, I worked throughout high school as a bagger in a grocery story, a clerk in a hardware store, a delivery driver for a dry cleaner, and an apprentice installer for the telephone company.

Project these practical lessons in the work ethic throughout a lifetime—and then bring labor to a screeching halt.

Psychologists tell us "habits become drives" over a period of time. To reverse the engines of a lifetime and go into neutral doesn't happen without grinding the gears and laying rubber on the road. I cannot understand retirees who quit work with a sigh of relief and feel content to become couch potatoes. For me, at least, the work ethic is a drive so deeply engrained that I feel guilty on Monday morning when everyone else is going to work. As a Depression baby, I learned that "making a living" is one of the values that defines who we are and what we are worth.

No wonder baby boomers, baby busters, and Generation Xers do not understand me! They know nothing about economic depression or rubber washers for hockey pucks. Born into a high-tech world of affluence, where making a living is assured, their driving force is to "make a life." Thus, work becomes secondary to relationships and survival gives way to significance.

In one sense, I envy them.

When I think back upon my school days, I realize that a Depression kid from a blue-collar family had few options for higher education or career. Corporate or civic leadership never came into my sights. My father often quipped, "I went through Harvard, in one door and out the other." My lot in life seemed set.

Sheer grit, hard work, and the grace of God took me to a college presidency—but even there, I found myself contending with Ivy Leaguers who confirmed my dad's other favorite saying: "You can always tell a Harvard man, but you can't tell him anything."

The New Leisure Ethic

Are we like Rip Van Winkle, who slept through a revolution? When he went to sleep, a picture of King George III hung on the wall. When he awakened, a portrait of George Washington had taken its place.

Have we slept through another revolution in American history? Two generations ago, the creed of the work ethic graced the wall: "Make a Living." Today, the leisure ethic has taken its place: "Get a Life."

The difference in these signs represents a revolution of American character that may rival the revolution of American freedom. In the first revolution, patriots declared independence, not just against the oppression of King George III, but against the English class system that separated citizens of high birth and wealth from laborers bound in poverty. Benjamin Franklin serves as the model of a man who rose from the printer's trade and became an esteemed citizen of the world. His *Poor Richard's Almanac* extols the virtues of the self-made person who rises to wealth and position by hard work and self-discipline. The Franklin model served us well into the twentieth century. His enterprising and egalitarian spirit is the image of America.

But if the leisure ethic has replaced the work ethic, does the Franklin model still motivate us? An even larger question is whether we have returned to a class system that grants special privilege to those who are born wealthy. If so, who is the model for the new American?

Not by accident, *all* of the 2004 candidates for the U.S. presidency and vice presidency (from both major parties) were multimillionaires. Perhaps their collective image portrays the ideal for twenty-first-century America.

What then are the virtues of this image that replace Franklin's hard work and self-discipline? Is it the motivation to "get a life" through relationships? Or is it the desire to do something significant with that life? Where does the current quest for spiritual reality fit in?

The new image on the wall is still a blur. As with all social upheavals, the post-revolutionary period of reconstruction makes final judgment on the virtues of the venture. If the current search for spirituality is any indicator, then the new leisure ethic has not trumped the old work ethic. Perhaps that is why I still watch the procession of cars heading for gridlock and ask, "Where is everyone going on Monday morning?"

4

What Do You Put
on Your Business Card?

A business card is a modern version of a six-shooter. Salespeople, armed with business cards, are masters of the quick draw.

One evening, my wife and I were dining at a crowded restaurant in the outskirts of Vancouver, B.C. Our table backed up against another table where a man, woman, and child sat eating. We paid no attention to them, but he paid attention to me. Somewhere in the conversation with my wife, I mentioned the need to get my watch fixed. When the man got up to leave, he thrust a business card at me with the comment, "You don't have to go downtown anymore. I fix watches right here in our neighborhood."

Totally surprised, I muttered, "Thanks," and read the details on the card about the name of the business, the identity of the owner, and the letters behind the man's name that identified him as a qualified watchmaker.

During my working days, my business card served me well. I used it to introduce myself when I visited foundations or corporations on fund-raising visits. When I worked the lobby of educational conferences, I traded cards with other delegates whom I met for the first time. Even on vacations, the business card became a connector with new friends we met at the pool or on a tour. Of course, I also dropped them through the slot in restaurants that had a weekly drawing for a free meal or in the glass jar on the motel counter that promised a new attaché case. But what should my card say *now*?

The Tenuous Title

A bulky file in my desk drawer contains fifty to sixty business cards that I have collected on my travels. Another drawer holds the history of my employment, according to the cards I kept. I have at least 500 from my last presidency and two other boxes contain cards from my days as the chair of two different boards of trustees.

Each time I try to throw them away, I feel as if I am discarding a part of myself. A good feeling washes over me when I look at a card and read, "David L. McKenna, President." In the succession of time, I am also identified as "Doctor," "Reverend," and "Chairman."

One by one, I retired from those titles. The only ones remaining are "President Emeritus, Asbury Theological Seminary," and "Chair Emeritus, Spring Arbor University."

The title "Emeritus" is dubious. Latin scholars can debate whether "E-meritus" means "with merit" or "without merit." One thing is sure: the titles of retirement have no authority, no function, no office, no administrative assistant, and no expense account.

So—what do I put on my business card in retirement?

On a regular basis, someone asks if I have a card, or requests come for a title by which I want to be known. One thought: to add "Ph.D" after my name. Or if excess vanity ruled, I would prepare a string of letters for my earned degrees: "B.A., M.Div., M.A., Ph.D." But then I remembered the critic who said that some Christians are trying to win the world by degrees. Even when I was in career, I refused to use the Ph.D. designation after my name on letterhead, annual reports, or business cards. Fishing for other options, I came up with the idea of "Author and Lecturer," but those words also seem self-serving. Later, I tried the catchall title of "Senior Consultant," but all of the bad jokes about consultants came to mind. Finally, I settled simply on the name, "David L. McKenna."

Only a few people from a past generation still call me "Dr. McKenna." Former students now greet me as "Dave," and kids in the neighborhood blow kisses at "Grandpa Dave."

Not much of a moniker for a business card.

The Naked Self

Retirement is a hard teacher. It is an ego blow to lose all of the titles by which we have been known for years. When Henri Nouwen moved from his professorship at Yale to his priesthood at Daybreak, a home for mentally-retarded individuals, he had the same experience. All of his degrees, honors, and titles of distinction disappeared in the befogged minds of simple people reaching out for love. Nouwen likens the experience to peeling the layers off an onion until nothing remains but his "naked self."[3]

In retirement, we learn what he means. During our careers, our identity tends to become inseparable from our title. When this happens, retirement is a threat that peels away our old identity, one layer at a time, until we are exposed in our "naked self." Some of us do not like what we see. Having played a given role for so long, we may lose our personhood to a title. Retirement, then, is misery.

To protect against this reality, some of us stay too long on the job; others invent alternative titles within the organization in order to preserve identity; and still others seek other jobs with high-sounding titles to avoid the specter of being a nonentity in retirement. Even the title of "greeter" at Wal-Mart or "crossing guard" at a school intersection gives a measure of dignity.

Tragic stories follow those who run out of options. After being forced into retirement, they wither and die, both inside and out. "Who am I in my naked self?" they ask. And too often they get only an empty answer.

The Identity Calamity

Retirement from institutions, roles, and titles leaves us no choice but to ask the question of the naked self. When all of our titles get stripped away, what is left?

We may find ourselves shallow, lonely, and (perhaps) unloved. This is more than an identity crisis; it is a *calamity*.

I recall a president who served long and well in the chief executive's role. But when he arrived at the stipulated retirement age, he pled with the board of directors for extension after extension. Finally, the board said no and he left, bitter and disillusioned. By the time his spirit had healed, his body had wasted away. Death came soon afterward.

In another instance, I had a professor friend whose wounded spirit in retirement tainted his distinguished career in the classroom. Some of his colleagues finally got to him in his mid-seventies, but only after his teaching had become a joke among the students. He finally left, kicking and screaming. The last time I saw him before his death, he groused about his lot in life, and especially resented the fact that he had been "put on the shelf" before his time. To borrow from C.S. Lewis's description of a person in hell, the grumbler had become a "grumble."

Retirement can do this to us. It is a catalyst for revealing the naked self.

When positions and titles drop away, we find out who we really are. Some retirees follow the path of the president into depression and early death. Others, however, grow larger in spirit and more vibrant in life as they age.

How do we account for the difference? At least one answer is found in our core identity. In retirement, our core identity, independent of titles and roles, is set free to grow. So a grumbler becomes a "grumble," a singer becomes a "song," a laugher becomes a "laugh," and a lover becomes "love."

In such cases, the self-identity of a person coming into retirement is predictable. We already know that the avocational interests cultivated by a person in career will carry over into retirement. Golfers will golf, runners will run, painters will paint, and travelers will travel. People who dream of doing new things in retirement usually are due for disappointment. By and large, we can invoke the rule that the avocational interests we cultivate in career will absorb more of our time and become more meaningful in retirement. Ask anyone who vows to start fishing, golfing, painting, or traveling *as soon as they have the time.* Most likely, in retirement, they are still vowing to start.

Can we say the same for the personal identity of the retiree? That is, whoever we are in career will be who are in retirement—only more so? Perhaps we are just like the first sentence in Tolstoy's novel *Anna Karenina*: "All happy families resemble one another, each unhappy family is unhappy in its own way."[4] If we are happy in career, then we will be most happy in retirement. If we are unhappy in career, then we be will most unhappy in retirement.

Count on it! Exposure of the naked self comes to all of us when the work ends, the position goes away, and the title gets removed. The proof is on our business card. When it reads nothing but our name, our identity has to stand on its own.

5

How Do You Suffer a Full-Time Spouse?

Everyone has heard the quip about the wife of a new retiree who complained, "I've got a full-time husband on one-third the salary." She was not speaking idle words.

Retirement is one of the toughest tests of marriage, especially after the husband and wife have established long-term patterns of interaction in which career occupies a big block of time and attention. In traditional gender roles the wife has an absentee husband during the week and a full-time husband on the weekend. With just the flash of a gold watch or the deposit of a severance check, the relationship shifts toward interdependence on a full-time, daily basis.

I used to think that retirement would be harder on me, the husband, but in truth, my wife had to make the greater adjustment. After all, a full-time husband invaded her domain.

Imagine what would happen if a wife moved into her husband's office as a full-time presence! It would be a disaster in the making. Yet when a man retires and becomes a full-time presence in the home, we assume that the adjustment required is minimal.

Just the opposite is true.

Despite years of anticipating retirement, the give-and-take of a successful marriage becomes more testy than ever. Imagine the added stress of a two-career family when both husband and wife retire! A whole new world awaits them.

Tell-tale Trends

I suspect that long-term trends in marriage, whether in a one-career or two-career family, get magnified by retirement. Little fights become big fights; little joys become big joys. As an observer of retired couples in the setting of a senior community, I have seen it all. In the checkout line at the supermarket, retired couples bicker about trivial matters, while on the golf course, retired couples become arch enemies. One gets the impression that the only bond between them is a pension check.

Right or wrong, let me offer an amateur's diagnosis for the "common grump" that ails some retirees. The couple has lost the common dream for their marriage and the individual dream for each other. Long-term marriage is a finely-tuned balance between togetherness and individuality. As Kahlil Gibran writes of marriage in *The Prophet*:

> You were born together, and together you shall be for evermore....
>
> But let there be spaces in your togetherness.
>
> And let the winds of the heavens dance between you.[5]

Before retirement, the common dream is natural. The couple shares the anticipation of building a home, raising the children, and succeeding in a career. One by one, these natural dreams are fulfilled and then closed down. The home becomes too big, the nest is empty, and the career is over. So with those common dreams behind us, we pose together the big question:

What now?

The same can be said for the individual dreams we have for each other. So often, the wife's dream for her husband is tied to his career, and the husband's dream for his wife is related to the home and family, with the possible intermixing of a career. Because our individual dreams so often are aimed at time-targeted goals, retirement is the tipping point when we also ask for each other, "What now?"

Could the answer to the question be found in the long-term trends established in marriage long before retirement? As strange as it seems, a married couple can *love* each other without *liking* each other. "Love" is the bond that weds a couple, builds a home, raises children, supports careers, and smoothes out differences. Still, lovers may not be friends. To be a friend is to enjoy each other's company when you are bound together on an inescapable, full-time basis.

The Lover's Test

My wife and I went through this friendship test on a 5,000-mile auto trip in Europe during the 1970s. Phil Smart, a friend in Seattle who owns a Mercedes dealership, invited us to pick up a new automobile at the factory in Stuttgart, drive it around Europe for the price of gas, and then leave it at Amsterdam for shipment home, where it could be sold to the advantage of both customer and dealer.

For the first time in our twenty-five years of marriage, my wife and I were stuck with each other in a confined space, seven days a week, twenty-four hours a day. Our luxury wheels took us to Munich, Milan, Florence, Monte Carlo, Nice, Marseille, Barcelona, Málaga, Toledo, and Madrid. As we headed north from Madrid toward France, the revelation came to me: "The woman next to me is not only my wife, my lover, and the mother of our children. She is also my best friend and buddy!"

Although we have different tastes in art and culture, respond from opposite styles of personality, and deal with issues in potentially conflicting ways, we enjoyed every moment we were together. If we wanted to talk, we did; but if we wanted to ride miles in silence, we could. With one mind and spirit, we looked forward to the next destination as an adventure.

In Toledo, Spain, for example, we arrived late without a hotel reservation. Trying to wend my way through the ancient part of the city, I drove the Mercedes down cobblestone streets with only a couple of inches to spare on each side (alarming when you're driving an automobile with a hand-rubbed finish). Janet suffered through every intersection as we crawled forward. Finally, we came out of the maze to a wide highway. By chance, I spotted the castlelike walls of a Spanish posada on the left and turned in. Although the windows were boarded, I knocked with the hope of an answer. A face appeared and I asked for a room. The luck of the draw was with me. A last-minute cancellation left one room open. Of course, we took it. Too tired to appreciate the grandeur of our surroundings, we checked into our room and fell asleep with a sigh of relief and prayer of gratitude.

In the morning, I got up and pushed out the wood-carved, double doors that led to the patio, and beheld a sight never to be duplicated. Our posada was perched high on a hill overlooking the fortress city of Toledo, with a deep gulley lying in between. The sun sparkled on the walls of our momentary Camelot and we found ourselves wafting on the wings of imagination as we embraced on the balcony. My cautious wife had survived my reckless spirit. We were buddies.

Looking back, I see that travel experience as boot camp for retirement. Today, we are almost inseparable. Although we often exercise the option to do our own thing, we anticipate coming back together again. So much so, that we have decided we no longer need two cars. It is more fun to go together or plan our schedules so that we can pick each other up. There is no negotiating on time limits or trade-offs of private time. After fifty-eight years of marriage and fourteen years of retirement, we love each other more and like each other best.

We are not only soul mates; we are friends.

6

Whatever Happened to Friday Night?

T.G.I.F — call it the acronym for a national obsession. One hears, "Thank God, it's Friday" as frequently as "good morning" on Monday.

I consider this a sad commentary on our attitude toward work and a sadder commentary on the separation of contemporary life into disconnected compartments. Lacking a rhythm of life that makes a symphony of the cycle of work, rest, worship, and play, we are left with conflicting fragments.

Naming Our Days

Many will remember the name of Colleen Townsend, a movie star who left Hollywood to marry the Rev. Dr. Louis Evans, Jr., senior pastor of the National Presbyterian Church in Washington, D.C. Their dual celebrity status launched them into the dizzy whirl of Washington society and their busy roles left little time for private moments. After a while, "Coke," as Colleen was known, put her foot down and declared one evening a week to be "Sweetie Night," to be spent alone with her husband. All other demands — no matter how urgent or prestigious — gave way to a private date of their own choosing.

My wife and I followed the Evans's example during the hectic years of presidential leadership. Two inviolable rules guided our relationship.

One: On Friday night Jan and I had a "date night." We went out together for dinner or stayed home and snuggled. In almost every case, we were not missed, or we found options to make up for our absence.

Two: Sunday evening was "family night." Although I could have been on the road for speaking engagements or conferences every weekend of the year, I choose to be home for church, family dinner, and rare evening together with the children for devotions, table conversation, and a review of the week ahead.

When you retire, the days become a blur. Without the familiar markers of going to work on Monday, getting over the hump on Wednesday, and thanking God for Friday, only Sunday remains to give us our bearings, since that's when we get up and go to church. Perhaps it is our compulsive drive for a schedule that leads us to restructure the week with daily identifiers.

Believe it or not, I frequently remember the days of the week by our luncheon routine. Monday, Wednesday, and Friday are special days for Chinese, Thai, and Mexican lunches. I also found myself marking the days of the week by favorite television programs, such as *The Practice* on Sunday, *Judging Amy* on Tuesday, and *The District* on Saturday. Because I hate to admit that my life might be media-driven, I re-created a schedule for weeding and trimming in the garden on certain days and doing the odd jobs of minor repairs and washing the car on other days.

Meanwhile, I find myself rebelling against appointments on-demand. Every week someone calls and wants to have coffee with me. I usually say yes, but when the time comes, I drag my feet. To be at any given place at any given time makes me feel as if I am back under the heel of a date book. It was bad enough when I lived by the thin day calendar in my breast pocket; now, when I see young executives pull out an electronic device to double-check their schedule, I pity them. Freedom of time is an asset of retirement that I prize. Even playing tennis, my favorite sport, makes me uncomfortable if I have to appear at a certain place at a specific time for a match.

Restoring Our Rhythm

Is this need to define my week by naming the days merely a leftover from a Depression-era work ethic? Or is it evidence of an offbeat in the rhythm of work, rest, worship, and play, brought on by retirement?

While in career, work is the dominant beat in the cycle. Rest is a counter-beat, while worship and play are accents. In retirement, however, work is reduced to a minor beat. For some, play takes dominance; for others, it is rest. Worship, in most cases, continues to be an accent.

So when work no longer defines our days, we must find substitutes. After observing retirees in a senior community whose days are defined primarily by play—such as golf or tennis—I believe that the cycle of work, rest, worship, and play must be continued throughout one's lifetime. The dominant beat in the rhythm may change, but a meaningful life depends upon the presence of all four beats.

I admire the retirees who work as greeters at Wal-Mart or crossing guards at intersections for grade-school children. Rather than seeing their task as menial, we should cheer their discovery of meaningful work in the cycle of a full life.

Irene, a retired woman in our neighborhood, is a devout Roman Catholic. Every morning she rises early to sing at morning Mass. Returning home, she walks several miles for exercise, rests in the afternoon, and entertains at night. She is one of the happiest retirees I know. Whether watching her walk down the street in the coordinated colors of her sweats, tennis shoes, and visored cap, or stopping to talk with her on the sidewalk, you can feel the rhythm of an abundant life.

Retirees, take note! The dominant beat of work that defined our days while we were in career may be diminished, but the beat does not disappear altogether. Some form of meaningful work must continue as part of the rhythm of life. The work may pay little or it may pay nothing, but it has to have meaning.

The Grace Note of Giving

The rhythm of life has another beat to which retirees must give attention. Our family history includes the story of an aunt who taught school for thirty years and then retired to Arizona. When a bond issue for school construction was proposed for her community, she led the senior-citizen opposition to the measure. The contradiction in her behavior escapes comprehension. This aunt, who was living off a generous pension from the public schools, argued that she should not have to pay for new schools because she had no children who would attend them!

Many retirees maintain the same attitude my aunt had. Churches, charities, and civic organizations that try to enlist them for gifts or volunteer services often get the answer, "I've paid my dues." Apparently, these retirees link charitable compassion to an active career as an obligation to be paid; but once the work is over, the retiree is entitled to rest, play, and drive a car with the bumper sticker, "We Are Spending Our Kids' Inheritance." They assume that the new generation of workers has the responsibility to carry the load of good deeds.

Whether they know it or not, retirees who think they have paid their dues are undermining the spirit of self-giving that is unique to our society. After G. K. Chesterton visited our nation early in the twentieth century, he returned to his home in England to write, "America is a nation with the soul of a church." If anyone should keep that spirit alive, it is the twenty-first-century retirees who are prime beneficiaries of that inheritance.

To the rhythm of work, rest, worship, and play we must add the verb *give*.

The psalmist writes, "Teach us to number our days aright, that we may gain a heart of wisdom" (Psalm 90:12). The verse refers to the discipline of time and contains a truth that applies to every generation and throughout one's lifetime.

Especially in retirement, we face the challenge of making the most of our days. By continuing the cycle of work, rest, worship, and play, we feel the rhythm of life. By adding the grace note of giving, we find the meaning of life. In this way, we gain a heart of wisdom, which is the goal of life.

7

What Do You Do with a Closet Full of Ties?

While climbing the ladder of career, my uniform for executive dress included a dark blue suit, a white shirt with a stiff collar, black wingtip shoes, and a rep tie with classic stripes. For official academic ceremonies, I put on the garb of my authority—a scholar's satin robe with velvet slashes on the sleeves, a doctoral hood displaying the maize and blue colors of the University of Michigan, a floppy velvet beret of Continental cut, and the presidential medallion.

Later, as I became more secure in my position, I added the semiformal uniform of a navy blue blazer, a button-down shirt, gray flannel slacks, and cordovan loafers. The classic rep tie, however, legitimized the outfit. Even when fashion changed from narrow to wide ties and back again, the stripes stayed the same.

I was like the guy who ate bologna-and-cheese sandwiches every day of his life. When he broke his jaw in an accident, he had to have it wired shut. Yet, he was so addicted to bologna-and-cheese sandwiches that he put them in a blender and sucked the liquid through a straw. I was equally addicted to rep ties.

Not until the middle of my career did I venture out to buy plain, printed, or patterned ties. Even then, I did not feel quite dressed for the academy.

Because of my boring executive uniform, I became a collector of quality ties. Under the rationale that a new tie was as good as a new suit, I bought ties for conferences, dinners, speaking engagements, anniversaries, birthdays, and often, just for personal whim. At least once a week, I took a mini-vacation after downtown lunches to scout the tie counter at Nordstrom. Clerks left me alone because they knew that they could not help me pick out a tie; but they also knew that if I saw one that struck my fancy, I was a buyer.

Cool by Collar

My tie-buying binges continued until the gala dinner given for my retirement. I went out in a blaze of color with a Robert Talbot "Best of Class" tie. A week later, Jan and I were on our way to Sun City, Nevada to join a community restricted to persons fifty-five years and older. The moving van followed with its load of furniture, household items, and personal effects, including a closet full of suits and ties.

What a change! Except for at church on Sunday, no one in Las Vegas wears a tie. Yet to indulge my addiction, I used Sunday worship and occasional speaking or consulting engagements as my excuse for buying a new tie.

When we moved to our retirement condo, I rediscovered two other artifacts of the tie-buying history. In a small box of collectibles, I found tie tacks that I used to wear. One was an onyx stone, another a tiger's eye, still another a gold tennis racket, and the prize of them all: a diamond-studded tie tack worn only by past presidents of Rotary.

Digging deeper into the box, I made my second discovery. Gold tie bars and tie pins brought to memory my frustration with the ties whose knots slipped crooked in the collar. When I picked up the solid gold tie pin I had received as a gift, I remembered that this little instrument of vanity had become the signature for my style of dress. These tie pins went through eyelets in the shirt collar to assure perfect alignment of the tie at all times.

My finding embarrassed me. Was I so vain that a crooked tie destroyed my self-esteem? Most of the Ivy League educators with whom I worked prided themselves in wrinkled button-downs and skewed ties.

I am convinced that uniforms of dress come in many colors, shapes, and styles. One thing is certain when I think about my tie bars and tie pins: I wouldn't be caught dead in those things again.

Skeletons in the Closet

The Salvation Army reaped a windfall when we moved back to Seattle — a city known for its "grunge" dress — and into a neighborhood of "techies" who worked at Microsoft, where ties are taboo. To wear a tie is a dead giveaway. You are either a visitor from back East, or a green recruit looking for a job.

Even in worship services, ties are as extinct as a dodo bird. Only at the dedication of a grandchild have I worn a tie. You can imagine why former students are shocked to see me in church on Sunday. My attire is a V-neck sweater and sport shirt, or turtleneck under a jacket. Even then, my dress seems formal compared to the holey jeans, tattered shorts, logo T-shirts, and grubby shoes of many worshipers. Church has robbed me of one of my greatest joys.

Oh, the dilemma! What do I do with a closet full of ties?

I don't dare count them, for fear of guilt. I don't want to give them to Goodwill, because I keep thinking that I will wear them again. So there they hang, waiting for the world to change.

Meanwhile, when I do wear a tie to some special event, I scour the rack and invariably choose one favorite tie. This makes me sad because it suggests that in retirement, I have become a one-dimensional character. Something has been lost—and I think I know what it is.

When I taught sociology to college freshmen many years ago, I always piqued their curiosity with the question, "When a man meets a woman, where does he look first?" After they laugh and giggle, I tell them that the answer is *her lips.* Then I turn the question around and ask, "When a woman meets a man, where does she look first?" The old answer used to be *his tie.* The color of a woman's lips and the stylishness of a man's tie were key points of attraction between the sexes.

Horrors! A woman still has lips to color, but what about the man without a tie? Where do the woman's eyes focus? Perhaps someone has researched the question, but I do not know the answer.

No matter how neat or colorful an open-necked shirt may be, in my opinion it is no match for a tie. Maybe that's why I still have a closest full of ties. I am waiting for them—along with my attractiveness to the opposite sex—to come back into style. Don't laugh!

I know it will be a long, long wait.

8

How Do You Say 'Hello' at Your Class Reunion?

Life is filled with awkward moments. The other night, my wife and I went to dinner with a dear friend and his wife, whom we had not seen for almost five years. When we met, he looked at me and burst out with the compliment, "You look *great!*" I did not know how to respond, so I resorted to my sarcastic wit: "Greater than what?"

My wife immediately stepped in. "Honey," she said, "Greg is paying you a compliment. Accept it."

Her wisdom set me thinking about the way in which we greet our aging friends.

The Diplomatic Dodge

Nothing is more awkward than the words that follow "Hello" at a class reunion. Whether the reunion is the tenth, twenty-fifth, or the fiftieth, we will be faced with the ultimate test of diplomacy.

Margaret Mead said that the final test for Britishers who go through their school of diplomacy is to say "thank you" for a gift they do not want. The same can be said for the compliments we receive at class reunions. How do we respond to gratuitous greetings from former classmates who try to be nice, even when they are not sincere?

Each time I think about going to a high school or college reunion, I remember the old story about the boy who lacked tact. Typically he would approach a girl at his high school with a blunt, "You are fat!" So his parents sent him to a school to learn how to be tactful. He completed the course and graduated with honors. His parents felt delighted that he had learned his lesson! But at his first dance after graduation, he complimented his partner by saying, "For a fat girl, you don't sweat much."

That's the way I feel about class reunions. Baldness, bulges, and bifocals characterize the men, while coiffeurs, calories, and cosmetics define the women. How do you tactfully say "hello" to your former classmates, who inevitably show the signs of aging? You have to couch a compliment in enough ambiguity to avoid a lie. Furthermore, you have to help your classmate respond without embarrassment.

After attending ten, twenty-five, and fifty-year reunions, I think I finally have the answer.

Dealing with Decades

Ten-year reunions are the least awkward. The most common greeting is, "You haven't aged a bit!" This is a gracious lie, of course, but it always works. It forces your classmate to respond by gushing, "Neither have you," or "You've got to be kidding." A second look will probably show some telltale signs of aging, although some people actually look younger as they age. At the ten-year reunion, however, you cannot go too far wrong with this compliment.

Twenty-five year reunions present an advanced challenge. Whether it is the twenty-fifth reunion from high school or college, age is beginning to take its toll. Men are going bald and getting bulgy; women are growing hippy and resorting to makeovers. How do you say "hello"? The most tactical greeting I know is to widen your eyes, put a little surprise on your face, and gush, "How do you stay so young?" On the surface, it appears to be the ultimate compliment. The immediate assumption is that "young" means the person hasn't changed at all. Deep down, however, we know that age takes a toll on all of us, especially as we hit the mid-forties and early fifties. Still, it is fun to play the game. When you ask, "How do you stay so young?" the answer will be a blush, a denial, and a struggle to return the compliment. "Thanks. You look great yourself. How do you do it?" is the most gracious response. And so goes the game. Anyone who would dare to tell the whole truth by saying to a man, "I didn't recognize you," or asking a woman, "How many children do you have?" flunks the test of tact.

Fifty-year reunions bring home the reality of aging with a vengeance. I remember giving a commencement address to a graduating class at a seminary where the fifty-year alums were also honored. As they struggled to their feet, leaned upon their canes, and pushed their wheelchairs to the front, I was aghast. They all looked as if they were on break from life support systems in the local nursing home. I chuckled to myself, because I remembered the story about the elderly lady who ran naked through the halls of the nursing home in full view of the other residents. When an old man was asked how he felt about what he saw, he answered, "I don't know, but whatever it was, it sure needed pressing."

Then, when the year of the class was announced, I choked on my chuckle. I was only one year away from the same fifty-year reunion!

I chose not to go back for the event.

Why did I stay home? For one thing, I did not want to be among those "old people." What would I say? "You look great for your age" would be a lie, while "Age has been kind to you" would border on an insult. So I stayed away.

No Need to Be Nice

The full reality of aging came to me after my fifty-fifth high school reunion (that I also missed). With diminishing numbers due to death and distance, the officers of the class concluded there should be no more reunions. So they closed the treasury and sent each of the remaining members a $30 check as our share of the distribution. I felt an ominous sense of finality when I received my check. Did this mean that we were waiting on each other to die?

Not me!

I applaud the veterans of the Normandy invasion and the bombers of Tokyo who still return to their reunions, even with diminishing numbers. It is enough that our youth culture is trying to make us old. I will stay as young as possible—physically, emotionally, and spiritually—so that I can still receive the compliment from those who tell me when I am ninety, "You look great!"

Who knows? I might even become what Gail Sheehy calls a "celebrating centenarian."[6]

PART **III**

Think Young

9

Is There Botox
for the Brain?

"Are you ready?" asked the advertiser. If so, then the remedy is Botox — the miracle drug for aging skin.

But hold everything! There is a catch. Botox injections "are not recommended" for people over the age of sixty-five.

Abraham Lincoln was right when he said that we cannot help the face we are born with, but after age forty, we have to live with the face we deserve. The same can be said for our wrinkles. After age sixty-five, apparently, we have to live with the skin we have.

The Glorious Quest

Despite the limits of age and the cost of its treatments, the popularity of Botox is another indicator of our continuing quest for the fountain of youth. Whether it is Ponce de León's sixteenth century crusade on the coast of Florida, searching for the healing waters of St. Augustine, or the Botox phenomenon of the twenty-first century, we will do whatever is necessary to restore our youth and resist the ravages of age. Just as people clamored for Lydia Pinkham's elixir when the medicine show came into town, so we will pursue any treatment that promises to make us young again.

Can we admit it? Behind the quest for eternal youth is the fear of inevitable death. Botox offers the illusion of a stop-gap measure against death, even if we know the results are temporary.

With so much attention given to preserving a youthful physical appearance, I wonder if there is Botox for the brain. I find the reality of mental decline more threatening than physical aging. When Jan and I lived in the retirement community of Sun City, we laughed at the "senior moments" when we lost our train of thought, forgot what we started to do, failed to remember the names of old friends, misplaced eyeglasses, or went to church wearing mismatched socks. None of us wants to admit that we are mentally dying a bit at a time.

But we are.

Better than Botox

There is another side to the coin. In my mind's eye, I see the image of Dr. Robert Fine, senior pastor of First Free Methodist Church in Seattle, Washington. I visited him in the hospital a few days before his death from colon cancer. Despite his emaciated face and jaundiced skin, his eyes flashed hope when he said, "Dave, my body is weakening—but I am so glad I learned to live in the world of ideas. The bed cannot confine me."

Dr. Fine is my model. As I age and live in retirement, I not only watch my diet and exercise my body to reduce cholesterol, but I also swallow vitamin E to help prevent Alzheimer's, compete with the estimated time for solving crossword puzzles, and explore creative options for the next stage of my writing while on my daily walk. Yet I find that this is not enough.

Is there anything like Botox that can jumpstart my intellect and keep it from excessive aging?

I found a possible answer in the book *Geeks and Geezers* by Warren Bennis and Robert Thomas. In their interviews with Geezers born after 1925 ("Depression babies"), they found evidence of "neotony" among many executive leaders. *Neotony* is a zoological term describing the process by which plants renew themselves. Transferred to executive leadership, Bennis and Thomas find aging "Geezers" who exude the fresh mind and vibrant spirit of youth. In fact, they can be characterized as persons who look out on the world with the curiosity and creativity of a child. Like a child, they awaken with eager anticipation to see what each new day will bring.[7]

When this refreshing outlook gets squeezed into its essence, neotony for the aging is a "sense of wonder." Walt Disney, even his later years, exhibited this. He was described as a person who looked out on the world with an "uncontaminated sense of wonder."

A Sense of Wonder

Is it possible that we have discovered Botox for the brain? If so, it is the biggest bargain on the market, because it costs nothing, needs no hype, and comes without negative side effects. All it requires is the wide-eyed wonder of a child.

To take a dose, go for a walk with a three-year-old child. A bug on the sidewalk warrants careful observation; a feather in the breeze dares to be chased; and a mud puddle waits to be sloshed. As Bennis and Thomas report, a Geezer who experiences neotony is a "first-class noticer."[8] Like a child, a Geezer awakens every morning with the anticipation of seeing what the day will bring.

Disney World, in Orlando, Florida, was not completed until after Walt Disney died. At the grand opening of the park, Walter Cronkite sat next to Disney's widow. As the celebration began, Cronkite said to Mrs. Disney, "It is too bad that Walter is not here to see this."

She shook her head and replied, "If he had not seen it first, we would not be seeing it now." Walt Disney gives the notion of neotony another childlike dimension.

A Shout of Joy

Students at Asbury Theological Seminary often hear the legendary story of Dr. J. C. McPheeters, who served as president from 1942 to 1962. "Doc," as he was known, always arose early in the morning to pray and memorize Scripture. Upon awakening, he immediately went to the window, threw back the drapes, and loudly exclaimed, "This is the day that the Lord has made; let us rejoice and be glad in it."

On one of his frequent trips across the country representing the seminary, he took a faculty member with him. They roomed together in hotels. True to form, Dr. McPheeters rose very early on the first morning, opened the drapes, and boomed with the voice of a camp meeting preacher, "This is the day that the Lord has made; let us rejoice and be glad in it." The sleepy faculty member heard reveille in the words, but turned over and went back to sleep.

When Dr. McPheeters greeted the morning on the second and third days of their travel in the same way, the faculty member finally got up the courage to suggest, "Dr. McPheeters, I appreciate the way that you praise the Lord every morning, but I need my sleep. Could you tone it down?"

The next morning, the faculty member sensed his president crawling out of bed, going to the window, and carefully opening the drapes. Then he heard him whisper softly, "This is the day the Lord has made, let us rejoice and be glad in it."

With such a joyous spirit anticipating the dawn of every day, no one will be surprised to learn about the exploits of Dr. McPheeters in retirement. He bought a speed boat at the age of seventy-six, took up water skiing two years later, slalomed twenty miles to celebrate his eightieth birthday, and into his nineties he demonstrated push-ups and weight lifting in an annual workshop for preachers. It took a massive stroke to stop him at the age of ninety-four.

Sooner or later, a sense of wonder becomes a shout of joy.

To greet each new day with joyous anticipation is like a shot of Botox for the brain and the soul. Even though I am not an early-morning person, when I take our little dog Molly for her walk to start the day, I sing to the ducks waddling on the grass and hum to the rhythm of the waters splashing on the shore, "Morning by morning, new mercies I see. All I have needed, his hand has provided. Great is thy faithfulness, Lord unto me."

There is no age limit on a sense of wonder. Retirees can stay young by awakening with anticipation, seeing with fascination, and noticing great things first.

Why not? Jesus told his disciples, "Unless you change and become like little children, you will never enter the kingdom of heaven" (Matthew 18:3). Long before zoology discovered neotony, Jesus gave the secret for refreshing our mind and re-creating our spirit. Even as we grow old, we can wake up every morning with the anticipation of seeing what the day will bring.

It may well be our first glimpse into the kingdom of heaven.

10

Who Wants to Drive
a Starter Casket?

Florida was our first choice for retirement. Our minds carried the memories of sunny skies, sandy beaches, shimmering seas, and billowing sails against the backdrop of painted sunsets. The scene changes, however, when you shift from the role of a short-term vacationer to a long-term retiree. We began to see Florida through different eyes.

As we toured housing developments along the canals leading to the Gulf, we could not help but notice the patios and pools screened to keep the bugs away. Wearing casual shirts and slacks rather than swimming suits, we learned what is meant by a "three-shirt day." The humidity almost choked us once we got away from the ocean.

But the signal that sent us packing for the West was the sight of snowbirds driving Cadillacs and Continentals with the bumper sticker, "We Are Spending Our Children's Inheritance." As if this red flag were not enough, women drove the cars while men rode along as passengers. Horrors!

The threat went beyond my macho image, all the way to my Detroit ancestry. I simply could not accept the idea of driving a "starter casket."

A Motor City Kid

Have patience with me while I retrace my Detroiter DNA. As far back in my childhood as I can remember, automobiles occupied an important place in my life. During the Depression, my dad loaded Ford engines on boxcars. Later, he uncovered his engineering skills as a draftsman for Motor State Products.

Even though Dad never finished high school, he developed those skills to become one of the top designers of convertible tops. With pride, I can point to the fact that he took the old, ugly mechanisms inside the convertible and fit them into a smooth "U" track along the inner edge of the newer models, so that the braces and bars actually disappeared. Even more pride shows when I tell our grandchildren that Grandpa McKenna transferred his genius for designing convertible tops on Ford Thunderbird autos to making hospital beds with automatic mechanisms to raise and lower the head and feet.

As you might expect, Dad drove a convertible. Except for my position as a college president, I would have driven one, too. In fact, I remember feeling envy when I heard that Carl Lundquist, a very conservative ministerial colleague and former president of Bethel College and Seminary, had created a stir on campus when he showed up one morning driving a fiery red Fiat convertible. The students promptly named it, "The Presidential Fiat."

Although I never dared to follow Carl, I confess that the desire to drive a convertible still lingers in my mind. Special encouragement came when I heard that the Mazda Miata was a favorite of "older" drivers. One Sunday afternoon, I sneaked into a Mazda lot to survey the field—but lacked the courage on Monday to make the purchase. Instead, I worked out my love for automobiles by driving the best car I could during my presidential years, and following my dad's advice, to trade every three years.

Trading in the Blood

When Jan and I got married, Jan's father surprised us with the gift of a brand-spanking new 1950 Chevrolet sedan that fed my natural desire. It cost only $1,000, but it was a beauty. We drove that gem to Vicksburg, Michigan, where we served as student pastors to a small and struggling Free Methodist Church.

Although we had a better automobile than any of our poor parishioners, no one ever complained. We continued to drive that car through our seminary days, but when we accepted our first faculty position at Spring Arbor Junior College, the "Motor City Bug" bit me again. I traded up for a 1953 Chevrolet. But that lasted only two years, ending when a drunk driver hit me broadside and almost totaled the car. From then on it drove like a dog going down the road skee-hawed.

So I traded again for a new, 1955 sports-model, four-door beauty that I guarded like a priceless gem. The results of all of my TLC disappeared, however, when I tried to take an ornery tomcat into the country while our daughter was away at school. No one ever told me that I needed to put the cat into a bag. Instead, I placed him in the back seat of my prized automobile. No sooner had I hit the road than the cat hit the car. Jumping from the back over my neck and across the seats, round and round he went, spraying his frustration all the way. I drove as fast as I could, but never reached my destination at a farm many miles away. Finally, unable to stand the smell, I braked the car, opened the door and kicked the cat out.

I traded *that* car soon after.

As a symbol of my advancement from the "Chevrolet" town of Spring Arbor Junior College to the "wide, wide world" of Ohio State University, I bought a new Oldsmobile. It served as the class act for my new position as assistant professor of higher education and director of the Center for the Study of Higher Education.

My only problem was that no one noticed.

So when I returned to Spring Arbor Junior College to serve as president, I retreated back to best-model, regular turn-around plan with a Chevrolet. All worked well until I moved to the Great Northwest. Suddenly, I encountered a world in which Japanese imports were valued over stateside products. A previously-despised Toyota came into view, but I finally settled upon an Audi as my presidential vehicle. Only later did I learn about the criticism that attended my decision.

Whether a German auto represented an act of treason, or its perceived cost represented an act of arrogance, I do not know. Perhaps that is why electronic demons attacked the car and rendered it useless. After endless trips to the garage, I decided that the machine was too smart for the mechanics.

A Lapse into Luxury

A seminary presidency presented its own unique automobile challenge. When I arrived at the position in Kentucky, I realized that I had changed worlds. Foreign cars, such as the Audi, gave way to Dodge and Ford pickups with bumper stickers reading "Made in America," along with CAT hats, CBs, gun-racks, and a German shepherd in the back. So, accepting reality, I opted for a Chrysler, already made famous by my predecessor.

Dr. J. C. McPheeters had the reputation of trading his Chrysler Imperial every year. When I arrived as president, he told me that he had put a dent in his newest Chrysler and didn't have time to wait for repairs, so he simply ordered a new one. I thought that I was home-free for trading automobiles every five years.

How wrong I was.

After trading a maintenance-prone Chrysler for an Acura Legend, I drove the car for five years. In 1993, the year before my retirement, I negotiated a deal with a Lexus agent that would let me turn over the Acura at a cheaper rate than it would take to buy a new Acura. Ecstatic with my deal, I drove the little Lexus home and to the office.

All hell broke loose.

One of those anonymous letters appeared from a student (or was it a faculty member?), accusing me of succumbing to the temptation of a "luxury" automobile. One look at the accusation, and I chose not to fight. The next day, I returned the Lexus with the commitment to pay whatever costs were involved, and ended up driving the Acura as the company car until the day I retired.

Guilty Pleasure

At our retirement dinner, everything changed again. As a parting gesture of gratitude, the board of trustees gave us a sizeable check with the instructions, "Buy the car you want."

This was like bait for a hungry fish.

After we retired, we made do with a Honda Prelude from our past, but found ourselves engulfed in the world of "starter caskets" from the retirees of Sun City, Nevada. Cadillac

DeVilles with leather roofs rule the day while Continental Town Cars with massive fenders rule the night.

One look at these automobiles (and their drivers) turns me off. *Under no circumstances* will I let my car become the symbol for advancing age and approaching death.

So, I began to do some research. One of the first things I learned is that the woman chooses the color and style while the man has his choice of engines. Next, I learned that personality is reflected in the color of the car. A white car is an ego trip drawing focus upon the driver, a red car is a hot-rodder's dream, and a black car is some kind of death wish. (Wisdom also says that a white car is a cooler car because it reflects the heat of the desert sun, while leather upholstery burns you in the summer and ices you in the winter.) The most important discovery, however, is to learn that certain automobiles betray the age of the owner. The current notion is that Mercedeses are driven by owners seventy years or older; Lexuses appeal to buyers in their sixties; and BMWs go to boomers in their forties or fifties.

Putting all of these facts together, I opted for the "guilty pleasure" of a white baby Benz or C-Class Mercedes. Fallacious as my reasoning may be, the car met Dad's standards for reliability and resale, Jan's wish for a white car, and my specious logic that a Mercedes is just another Chrysler product (at least, at the time of this writing). Ego, of course, reigns as we drive around the streets with a car that can never be mistaken for the "starter casket." As a small, zippy, and stylish car parked next to large, sluggish, and ugly monsters, it makes its own statement about our rebellion against aging by automobile.

Of course, my decision has a downside. Contrary to the Detroit mentality that touts planned obsolescence, a Mercedes gets better with age and holds its value. So, five years later, I have a pristine automobile with limited mileage that qualifies as "perfect" in Kelley Blue Book.

So what do I do now? My Detroit mentality says I should trade a five-year-old car, but my Seattle mindset says I should drive it until it becomes a "classic."

I know which mindset will win. After pushing and pulling between Detroit and Seattle, I will drive it for another five years, with my eye on the goal of buying a convertible for my eightieth birthday.

11

Shall I Climb Mt. Rainier
or Take a Cruise?

I admire George Herbert Walker Bush. To celebrate his seventy-eighth birthday, he skydived alone. He wanted to repeat the performance on his eightieth birthday, but they made him jump in tandem with two instructors.

Few of us will match his feat.

Go-Go Aspirations

You have already met a man named Julian Chester McPheeters. He was President of Asbury Theological Seminary when I was a student there in the 1950s. When I assumed the presidency in 1982, he was still traveling back and forth across the country as the chief ambassador of the seminary.

"Dr. Mac," as he was known, was a physical-fitness buff. At the age of seventy-eight, he took up water-skiing. To celebrate his eightieth birthday, he slalomed twenty miles on one ski. By the time I arrived on campus, he was in his early nineties and working out every day. So it seemed appropriate to give him a spot on the program of the annual ministers' conference to demonstrate the importance of physical fitness as a companion to spiritual fitness. I can still see him on the floor in front of the platform, lifting weights and urging fat pastors to get toned up physically and spiritually.

Everyone brings into retirement certain aspirations for physical feats, each feat usually some personal expression of *Fear Factor*. Mine included parasailing, scuba diving, and climbing Mt. Rainier.

I achieved the first goal by parasailing over the bay in Ocho Rios, Jamaica. My initial fears vanished as gentle winds lifted me off the dock and carried me high above the bay. Then, when the winds picked up, I looked down to see that I was actually pulling the speedboat backward through the water. The parasailing company hurriedly got me down and stopped all rides for the day.

A year or two later, I pretested my aspiration to dive deep into the ocean by snorkeling in the China Sea. With my attention fixed on the schools of colorful fish swimming beneath me, I failed to notice a giant jellyfish that decided to wrap itself around my thigh and sting my wetsuit with its suckers. By the time I beat the black beast off my leg and made it to the shore, I decided that I needed to concentrate on my supreme goal—climbing Mt. Rainier.

Residents of Seattle get periodically challenged by the sight of Mt. Rainier peeking through the clouds. On rare occasions, it towers over the city like a gigantic ice cream cone. Visitors feel enticed to drive up the mountain to Paradise Lodge and take a short hike along the trails. Real Northwesterners, however, want to brag about climbing the 14,000-foot mountain and then prove their story with a photograph of them taken at the summit.

My fascination with the mountain began with a story that a friend told me during a downtown Rotary luncheon. With a straight face and serious tone, he spun the yarn about a Seattle-ite who decided to climb Mt. Rainier. Prior to the climb, the man spent six months getting physically ready for the venture—toning muscles, strengthening legs, and improving breathing. Then, he went out and bought the best of climbing gear—waterproof parka and pants, spiked boots, fleece-lined gloves, UV-protection goggles, and whatever else goes with a high-priced outfit. He hired a guide and started the climb. Despite his conditioning, he ran out of steam and struggled with his breath as he entered the final stretch toward the summit. Suddenly, into his vision came what had to be a mirage triggered by his fatigue. Coming toward him was the proverbial "little old lady," in tennis shoes, leading a white poodle down the mountain! I suspect that my friend's story belongs in the category of snipe hunts and Sasquatch sightings, but regardless of its truth, my passion for the climb lost a bit of its fervor that day.

Aging took care of the rest.

After I retired, I took one more look at the requirements for climbing; it fatigued me just to read them. Then when I remembered the risks of climbing, fear joined fatigue. Admittedly, I had lost a step on the tennis court and puffed up little hills when I jogged, but the mountain suddenly loomed like a monster. Heart surgery then gave me my excuse and taught me another lasting lesson.

As we retire and age, we go through three stages: "Go-Go," "Slow-Go," and "No-Go." In the Go-Go stage, we entertain the notion that we can still compete at the peak level of our physical performance. To prove the point, we plan to parasail, scuba dive, and climb mountains. Sometimes it works out. The stories of marathon runners, skydivers, and mountain climbers in their sixties, seventies, and even eighties dare us to do the same. Yet statistically, these people fall at the far end of the bell-shaped curve. Most of us make up the hump in the middle — our aspirations exceeding our qualifications. The old saying proves right: "Our get-up-and-go is get-up-and-gone."

Slow-Go Adjustments

Age and circumstance give us a rough introduction into the Slow-Go stage. In my case, a heart attack slowed *everything* down. Instead of jogging four miles a day, I rallied to walk and run in short segments. My mind was still Go-Go, but my body wouldn't obey.

On the tennis court, I still had the vision of put-away shots that would win the point; but somehow, I missed the line or hit the net. Finally, after many misses, I learned that I had to change my tactics and lower the level of my competition.

After a while, things got even slower as I gave up running and settled for the comfort of knowing that a thirty-minute daily walk cuts the chances of another heart attack in half. Am I rationalizing my change in exercise? Of course, but I know that I am playing the percentages.

The fantasy of climbing Mt. Rainier has given way to the Slow-Go adventure of taking a cruise. Oh, the rigors of this adventure! The steepest climb is up the gangplank, the major exercise is pushing away from the table, the competitive climate is walking laps around the promenade deck, and the discipline is going to bed rather than eating dessert at midnight.

After taking a couple of cruises, we were cruised out for a while. Even though I could no longer indulge my fantasy of climbing Mt. Rainier, I needed a creative challenge as the substitute. You will never guess the Slow-Go fantasy that took its place. Like so many wishful dreams, it grew out of my religious background.

When I was young, I took piano lessons for more than ten years. In college, I picked up lessons again, but my playing remained limited to classical music and hymns. In my junior high gym classes, we were required to learn ballroom dancing. My parents wrote a note to the principal that got me out of these classes because of our religious convictions. And in my preteen years, my grandma, sister, and I were playing the "Authors" card game. Father entered the room, saw the cards, and took them away from us with the stern warning that we should *never* play with any kind of cards again.

So can you guess the fantasy that took the place of climbing Mt. Rainier? My Slow-Go fantasy is to learn jazz piano, ballroom dancing, and bridge! Admittedly, you burn fewer calories in these activities than in climbing a mountain. But think of the glee that comes with the dream of filling in the gaps of your youth and being free from the guilt that once went with these pleasures.

To date, I have not fulfilled any of these wishes, but the motivation of a fantasy has value in itself. I keep thinking that the breakthrough is just ahead. Come to think of it, there may be a fantasy cruise to match my fantasy lessons. If so, I might reverse the engines and just say, "bon voyage!"

Slow-Go may not be Go-Go, but it is better than No-Go.

No-Go Facts

Why do we assume that we will escape the No-Go stage? As with death and taxes, the No-Go stage is inevitable.

Just this morning on our thirty-minute walk, Jan and I passed a bent-over man who struggled with every step. As we passed him, he said, "Please go on. I am not very fast."

Reluctantly, I saw myself in him.

I threw back my shoulders and quickened my pace, determined to stay Slow-Go as long as possible. But really, who am I kidding? My pace *will* slow, my shoulders *will* slump, and I *will* join the company of those for whom Go-Go has descended to Slow-Go on its way to No-Go. In this stage, even a game of Scrabble becomes a spectator sport.

Is this despairing? Yes, if we assume that this life promises us immortality. No, if we accept our mortality and find new life in different dimensions.

Isn't this what the apostle Paul meant when he said, "To live is Christ and to die is gain"? If descending through the stages from Go-Go through Slow-Go to No-Go is decline, then we are the losers. But if the downward stages of physical strength and psychological ambition provide entry into another world—richer and fuller than the past—then we are the winners.

That is why, when I come to deciding between mountain climbs and cruise ships, there is no contest. I now choose the self-indulgent alternative of putting my luggage on board and letting the cabin steward worry about it.

Of course, I have my regrets because I never climbed Mt. Rainier. But I *have* climbed other mountains and stood on their summits. Life is like that. Rather than regretting what we have not done, we must celebrate the moments when we *have* planted our flag on the top of our aspirations and looked down upon the magnificent vista that rewarded our climb.

12

Where Are the Kid-Eating Bears When We Need Them?

It is not the kind of story that you tell your grandkids to put them to sleep. In the Old Testament book of 2 Kings, Elisha is walking along the road toward Bethel. A large band of rabble-rousing youth come out of the town and jeer, "Go on up, you baldhead!" The prophet turns around, stares at them, and calls down a curse on them in the name of the Lord. Instantly, two bears spring out of the woods, spot the jeering youth, and maul forty-two of them.

The moral of the story? Don't mess with the elderly.

What's In a Word?

Who can doubt that we are living in a culture geared to youth? When advertisers were asked to give the code words for selling their products, they answered, *young, free, pure,* and *new.* The opposite words are *old, bound, tainted,* and *used.* You do not need to be paranoid to know that the negative words are attitudinally attached to aging people.

Ask someone, for example, what word they associate with "old." "Old folks" would probably lead the way, followed by a string that might include "old age," "old man," "old woman," "old duffer," "old codger," "old geezer," "old bat," "old dog," "old nag," "old shoe." Try as I might, I could not find one noun with positive meaning that went with the adjective *old* in relation to a person. The affirmations of "Old Glory," "Old Ironsides," "old town," or "Old Blue Eyes" do not count.

If this were Old Testament times, the bears would have a feast.

Perhaps this why we work so hard to give negative terms a positive spin. Garbage collectors become sanitation engineers, store clerks become sales associates, and real estate agents become marketing and investment specialists. Naturally, then, calling people "old," "elderly," and "aged" has to give way to calling these people "seniors," a term that implies status and seniority. The other day, I ran across the term "elder-friendly" as a descriptor for a product that accommodated the needs of senior citizens. Today, when an aging movie star wants to justify her affair with a kid just a little older than her own children, the media picks up the cue and announces that "forty is the new thirty" in order to take advancing years off her life. I expect we will next see something like "chronologically-challenged" or "age-sensitive" in a vain attempt to cancel out the stigma of being "old."

It is also intended to keep the bears away.

What's With Our Age?

What's going on? At the same time that we are being accused of "age denial" in our pursuits to stay young, our culture is guilty of "age discrimination." The prejudice begins when age dictates our rights or privileges.

You must be eighteen to vote, twenty-one to drink, thirty-five to run for president, fifty-five to get senior discounts, fifty-nine to withdraw from IRAs without penalty, sixty-two to qualify for Social Security benefits, and seventy-and-a-half to start mandatory minimum withdrawals from your pension funds.

Informal discrimination is much more subtle. Many people in their teens and twenties don't trust those over thirty, and consider those past forty over-the-hill. A person is past the halfway point of life at fifty, expected to retire at sixty-five, close to the biblical limit at seventy, and eligible for an Elderhostel discount at eighty. With each age marker we feel the press of time and the onset of aging.

After that, discrimination becomes tolerance for repeated stories, corny jokes, falling asleep, using a cane, gaining weight, staying home, forgetting names, being cranky, spilling milk, drinking decaf, using the television's closed-caption option, leaving a tip of less than 15 percent, not worrying about carbohydrate consumption, lying about age, using a toothpick in public, flirting with store clerks, driving below the speed limit, choosing handicapped parking, napping at midday, and saying, "When I was your age...."

What Is Old?

One day I sat down to write my own definition of being "old." I decided you are old when you:

- Focus on yourself
- Fixate on the "Good Old Days"
- Complain that life is unfair
- Let sickness dictate your attitude
- Persevere on trivia
- Laugh little
- See more sin than grace

- Wallow in boredom
- Envy the young
- Give the devil more than his due
- Ignore babies
- Think that you have seen everything under the sun
- Dull the growing edge
- Fail to hum a happy tune
- Dread awakening to a new day
- Fail to see the wonders of the commonplace
- Tell one story over and over again
- Become a perpetual grouch
- Kick a dog
- Close your mind to a new idea
- Quit reading
- Pray with a woeful sound

I am probably prejudiced, but when I apply these criteria to my own outlook on life, I don't believe that I am old.

An Exception for Kids

Those who fear growing old use the tool of age discrimination. At the other extreme are innocent kids whose perceptions of aging are totally forgiveable.

When my wife and I retired to Sun City, Nevada, a friend sent us the following e-mail expressing an anonymous kid's viewpoint on retirement and a place like Sun City. It came under the title, "All About Retirement (From a Child's Point of View)." Once again, we hear truth from the mouths of babes:

After the Christmas break, a teacher asked her young pupils how they spent their holiday. One small boy wrote:

"We always used to spend Christmas with Grandpa and Grandma. They used to live here, in a big, brick house, but Grandpa got retarded and they moved to Nevada. Now they live in a place with a lot of retarded people. They all live in little tin boxes. They ride three wheeled tricycles and they all wear nametags because they don't know who they are all of the time. They go to a big building called a wrecked hall, but they got it fixed because it is all right now. They play games and do exercises there, but they do them very good. There is a swimming pool there. They go into it and just stand there with their hats on. I guess they don't know how to swim.

"As you go in their park, there is a dollhouse with a little man sitting in it. He watches all day so they can't go out without him seeing them. When they sneak out they go to the beach and pick up shells.

"My Grandma used to bake cookies and stuff, but I guess she forgot how. Nobody cooks, they just eat out. They eat the same thing every night, early birds. Some of the people are so retarded that they don't know how to cook at all, so my Grandma and Grandpa bring food into the wrecked hall and they call it potluck.

"Grandma says that Grandpa worked all his life and earned his retardment. I wish they would move back up here. I guess the man in the dollhouse won't let them out."

The child who wrote this will never have to worry about kid-eating bears. The story is too honest and the picture too realistic. Every "retardee" will have to laugh.

A List to Beat All Lists

So here is my confession. I conquer age by confessing my age. For what it is worth, at seventy-eight, I have reached the age when:

- My arthritis makes it less likely that I will lose my wedding ring
- My morning's work is taking out the garbage
- My discounts apply at Elderhostels
- My crimes are not likely to be punished by death
- My road rage is expressed only when I encounter young women driving while talking on cell phones
- My grandchildren are impressed that I lived in the twentieth century
- My wooden tennis racket is on display at the Smithsonian
- My expanding middle gives my wife more to love
- My slippers stay on most of the day
- My golf scores equal my age — for nine holes
- My dinners out are at the "early bird" time
- My chances of being kidnapped for ransom are drastically reduced
- My television set is permanently on closed caption
- My nonconformity is written off as senility
- My weekly calendar is on my pill box
- My stories are tolerated as oral history
- My high school will hold no more reunions

- My eyes close automatically after lunch
- My enemies are dying one by one
- My prescription antacid is now available over the counter
- My color is permanently winter on the palette of the seasons
- My wife still snores, but I can't hear it
- My new hobby is reading medical research
- My joints offer a more accurate forecast than the National Weather Service
- My Christmas presents no longer require batteries or need to be assembled
- My software will be upgraded only under duress
- My nitroglycerine is not used for making bombs
- My closet is filled with suits and ties waiting to come back into style
- My Palm Pilot has no entries

Up with age! People who are sixty-five and older represent the fastest-growing cohort in the total population. *Someone* needs to take us seriously. We can handle the jokes about aging and even laugh at ourselves—but when basic human needs are at stake, it is no laughing matter.

When Is Old, Too Old?

From time to time, serious attempts are made to charge senior citizens for the disproportionate share of governmental support they get through Social Security, Medicare, and Medicaid programs. Amitai Etzioni, a professor at The George Washington University, writes in *The American Scholar* of being asked to join a group called Americans for Generational Equity (AGE).[9] The group intends to oppose the American Association for Retired Persons (AARP) and seek a reduction in funding for senior citizens, in favor of children and youth. They appear motivated by the idea that elderly people do not deserve government support because they no longer make a contribution to the society.

Some advocates of this position go so far as to say to our seniors, "Settle your affairs and get ready to die." The role of government, in their view, is not to sustain quality of life by such programs as Social Security and Medicare, but only to make senior citizens "comfortable" in their last days.

Etzioni refuses to become a member of AGE because he sees through the ethical fallacy in assuming that elderly people have no contribution to make to society or deserve no support for past contributions. Christian ethicists will go a step farther to point out that the worth of human life is measured by more than biological age or economic prowess. In the biblical view of aging, seniors contribute memory to the community, wisdom to the contemporary experience, depth to spiritual understanding, and dreams for the next generation. Although the pro-life movement has not taken a strong stand on this viewpoint, it needs to be part of the "seamless garment" that represents the image of God in us.

AGE cannot be totally discounted, however. Politicians wink and nod when we appeal for medical coverage, long-term health care, and prescriptions for senior citizens. The same attitude persists when the statistics show millions of children without adequate housing, food, clothing, and health care. It is a blight on our society when elders of poverty join with children of poverty as the two poorest groups among us. Ironically, the political platforms of Democrats and Republicans always include a strong plank for health care; but when the election ends, the needs get lost in other priorities, embroiled in ideological factions, or buried under a landslide of contributions from political action committees.

But the issue will not go away. Baby boomers coming to retirement will soon swell the ranks of a graying population. Hordes of them were rebels of their own at an earlier age. So watch out! The boomers bring with them the experience of protest against the Vietnam war. As new retirees on the march for health care, their rallying cry might well be, "Seniors of the States, unite. You have nothing to lose but your pains." When that time comes, bears will no longer be needed. Yesterday's boomers are tomorrow's "baldies."

13

Do You Approve
this Message, Bob Dole?

Bob Dole got my vote for president, but I question his judgment in becoming a huckster for Viagra. After all of his years of eloquent speeches in leading the Senate, he may best be remembered by the sound bite, "I am Bob Dole and I approve this message."

I feel mixed emotions when I see Bob Dole stumping for Viagra. On one hand, I applaud his candor in confronting the handicap of erectile dysfunction. With a premium upon sexual performance in our society, he gives a ray of hope for every male who suffers from the malady. On the other hand, I wonder whether Bob Dole has sacrificed his wife, Elizabeth, on the altar of a million-dollar payout. I know that money motivates politicians, but at what price? Somehow, his endorsement of Viagra is not in sync with his reputation as an elder statesman who has a dour sense of humor.

Gladiators of Sexuality

As a retired person going through the process of aging, I have another beef against Bob Dole's hucksterism. It is one thing to tout the magic of a drug that restores potency to men who have lost the ability to perform sexually. But it is quite another thing to enter the arena where the winners are gladiators of enhanced sexual performance.

This plays directly into the hands of those who align happiness with youthfulness. To prove the point, take a look at the splash of ads on television for Viagra, Cialis, and Levitra. The malady of erectile dysfunction has given way to the wonders of enhanced and prolonged sexual performance. Young and vibrant middle-agers smile at us with the satisfaction of multi-orgasms. After a while, you feel like the cow in the field watching a milk truck driving by with bold letters on the side, reading "PASTEURIZED, HOMOGENIZED, FAT-FREE MILK." The poor cow turned to her companion on the fence row and mooed, "Makes you feel inadequate, doesn't it?"

As one of the older set following Bob Dole into the 1970s, I appreciate the promise of sexual rejuvenation. After heart surgery and a daily dose of drugs, I understand the warning about the loss of libido when sexual stimulation doesn't pass from the brain to the rest of the body. Surely, a little blue pill called Viagra will jumpstart the system and make me feel young again! All is well and good—until I do a double-take on reality.

It is one thing to enhance potency and quite another thing to put a premium upon performance. Television, movies, and novels idolize young studs who brag about their macho prowess for prolonged sex and multiple orgasms. Like lifting weights, sexuality is reduced to a contest of conditioning, with the partner spotting the success. Love and commitment play no part when good sex depends merely upon the best performance.

I also wonder if the wisdom of the body gets thrown out of balance by the sudden surge of sexual energy. When my wife's father was approaching eighty, his mind began to fail him. A medical examination found his carotid artery had clogged. So, using the medical equivalent of a Roto-Rooter machine, the doctor opened up the artery. The results were marvelous—Dad's mind cleared and he began to think like a fifty-year-old man again. Soon, however, it became apparent that his aging body could not match the expectations of his mind. Dad became frustrated with his life and groused about age. As protection against his dissatisfaction, Mom retreated into the protective shell of her own dementia. Both lived into their nineties, but with Dad's unhappiness and Mom's senility.

This experience led me to wonder about the wisdom of the body, not just as a fine-tuned organism when it is healthy, but also as a well-balanced unit of mind, body, and soul during the aging process. What effect does a pill for sexual performance have upon the rest of the body, to say nothing about the mind and soul? While I have no answer, Dad's experience raises the question. Are our bodies, minds, and souls intended to remain in balance when we age, just as they worked together during our youth?

Even more serious is the separation of sexuality from intimacy. It is true that Viagra, Cialis, and Levitra can enhance intimacy—but not unless intimacy already exists for the married couple. Gale Sheehy, in her book *New Passages*, diagrams what she calls "the Sexual Diamond."[10] At the top of the diamond are boys and girls up to the age of ten, whose sexuality is very similar. At puberty, the two sides of the diamond begin to diverge until men and women in their thirties are quite different sexually. In the fifties, however, the two sides converge again to form the bottom point of the diamond. These years (and those to follow in retirement and old age) are characterized by an intertwining of sexual desires for men and women.

Both want the qualities of intimacy—togetherness, gentleness, and interdependence. A snuggle can be as meaningful as sex.

I believe that Christians have a corner on intimacy. We know the meaning of the larger relationship within which sexuality exists. Beginning with the loving prayer, "Abba, Father," extending to the mystery of being "in Christ," and reaching out to the promise of becoming "one in the body of Christ," we celebrate the wonder and joy of intimacy. Without diminishing our sexuality or forfeiting our individuality, Christians bring the same love, mystery, and promise to the marriage relationship. Rather than cheapening our sexuality in competitive performance of counting orgasms, we view sex as an integral expression of the mystical union to which we give our pledge in our marriage vows. No matter how long we have been married, sex is still a mystery that cannot be fathomed.

Far beyond physical curiosity, it is spiritual discovery. It is filled with surprises because it is spontaneous. How else can you explain the beating of my heart when my wife drives out to the store? I can't wait for her to get back. Say what you like, but no pills can stimulate this response. It is a relationship so deep that it defies explanation.

Never say that intimacy lacks passion! While the passion may not be the white-hot surge of sexual desire, it is the steady glow of total commitment.

Champions of Intimacy

As Bob Dole has championed sexual rejuvenation, so we Christians need to champion intimacy. Someone needs to send the media message that sexuality is a small part of a larger package. To be intimate is to put sex into perspective. It is a grace note in the joy of life, but it is not the major chord that gives the symphony its lasting theme.

Retirement opens the door for the discovery of intimacy, and aging brings it to fullness. Best of all, intimacy does not have to be preplanned, with time limits on maximum performance. It just grows with the natural flow of life. So why not call it by its name?

Intimacy is **love** at its best.

Bob Dole: Do you approve *this* message?

14

Can Old Dogs Learn New Tricks?

Who says you can't teach old dogs new tricks? Most likely it's young pups who think that they know it all.

If you can't teach old dogs new tricks, I have lied to thousands of graduates at thirty-three commencements at which I have presided as president, and almost one hundred times when I have given commencements at other institutions. Why? *Because "life-long learning" is the passionate theme that I have preached from my bully pulpit as an educator.* Countless students have heard me say, "The real test of your education is whether you have gained a love for learning that lasts a lifetime."

My challenge is not limited by retirement or canceled by advancing age. Not only *can* old dogs learn new tricks; we *must* learn them to stay fully alive.

A Gleam in the Eye

As I recall, it was the president of Yale University who said, "A college campus is one of the few places in the world where you can still follow the gleam in your eye." Retirement is another of those "few places." This means that we can stay young as long as we are alive.

The late Pope John Paul II told a gathering of youth, "I am a young person in an eighty-three-year-old body." I like that! The most miserable and boring people I know are those who have lost the youthful gleam in their eyes, and with it the insights of new learning.

It is a false assumption that the learning curve goes into sharp decline with age. If anything, we can expect that the lessons of experience combine with reflective insights to produce a practical wisdom reserved for the aged. Everyone has heard about famous people who made their greatest contribution late in life, but the specific examples found in the little book *1,003 Great Things about Getting Older* are worth repeating:[11]

- Emily Post was in her fifties when she wrote her first book on etiquette.
- Harry Truman was first elected to the Senate at the age of fifty.
- Daniel Defoe did not start writing until he was almost sixty.
- Paul Cezanne held the first major exhibit of his art at the age of sixty-five.
- Ronald Reagan was elected to his second term as president at the age of seventy-three.
- Nelson Mandela became president of South Africa at the age of seventy-five.
- Grandma Moses gave up embroidery for painting at the age of seventy-six.
- Winston Churchill became prime minister of Britain at the age of seventy-seven.

The latest of these ageless wonders comes from the unlikely world of professional football. Years ago, Red

McCombs acted upon an impulse to buy the slumping franchise of the Minnesota Vikings for his own birthday present. When he surprised his wife with the announcement, she said, "Are you crazy?"

"No," Red answered, "I'm seventy!"

The point behind the stories is that none of these people stopped learning or leaping as they grew older. They also take away our excuses for cutting out our reading, crimping our imagination, refusing to listen, settling for small talk on a park bench, or not daring to take a risk.

What Age Teaches Us

Seriousness aside, it is good to stop and laugh at what we learn as we age. To celebrate his fiftieth birthday, Dave Barry, the nationally syndicated columnist, wrote a book titled *Dave Barry Turns 50*.[12] With his typical wit and whimsy, Barry tells us twenty-five lessons he has learned after reaching the half-century mark. Among his lessons are these ten gems:

- Never, under any circumstances, take a sleeping pill and a laxative on the same night.
- If you had to identify, in one word, the reason why the human race has not achieved, and never will achieve, its full potential, the word would be *meetings*.
- There is a very fine line between "hobby" and "mental illness."
- People who want to share their religious views with you almost never want you to share yours with them.
- You should not confuse your career with life.
- Nobody cares if you can't dance well. Just get up and dance.

- Never lick a steak knife.
- The most destructive force in the universe is gossip.
- You will never find anybody who can give you a clear and compelling reason why we observe daylight savings time.
- Never be afraid to try something new. Remember that a lone amateur built the Ark. A large group of professionals built the Titanic.

After chuckling over Barry's list, I decided that, as a man who just celebrated his seventy-fifth birthday, I should make a list of advanced learning. What difference does another twenty-five years make? For one thing, it greatly increases the list of lessons learned. For another thing, Dave Barry's list consists of hypothetical scenarios bathed in good humor. My list is a confession of stupid mistakes from which I have learned. Here they are:

- Never drink coffee after noon.
- Never ask anyone, "Have you read my book?"
- Never tell your grandchildren, "When I was your age…."
- Never doubt that bottle of Tabasco will last a lifetime.
- Never challenge a four-year-old to a video game.
- Never answer "yes" when someone stops in the middle of a joke to ask, "Have you heard this one?"
- Never let press clippings make you a legend in your own mind.
- Never buy bright lights for the bathroom mirror.

- Never start a project that requires a trip to the hardware store.
- Never go to Costco without a list.
- Never ask the doctor, "If I were your son, what would you do?"
- Never assume that blue means a baby boy.
- Never deny a woman who says that she has nothing to wear.
- Never expect a grandchild to laugh at your jokes.
- Never volunteer for overnight babysitting.
- Never assume that anyone who asks, "How are you?" really wants to know.
- Never waste the opportunity to take a nap.
- Never congratulate a fat lady on being pregnant.
- Never put something in God's hands and then take it back.
- Never say "never."

While these lessons may seem simplistic, they are not. Underneath the humor lies solid spiritual reality.

- Have we accepted the fact that we are mortal?
- Have we confessed that God alone is perfect?
- Have we admitted that we are sinful?
- Have we acknowledged our debt to grace?
- Have we learned to forgive others?
- Have we put our hope on the resurrection?

Life is not as complex as we make it. As we age, we need to laugh and learn from our stupid mistakes. We also need to learn from and loathe our stubborn ways.

More than forty years ago, I started keeping a daybook in my breast pocket for scheduling appointments and keeping a journal of quotes, jokes, prayers, praises, hurts, and lessons learned. Periodically, I go back to those little leather-bound books to check a date or an event. When I do, I also thumb through the pages to see how I felt and what I learned during those days. It is an experience of mixed emotions. Sometimes I laugh; sometimes I weep; sometimes I praise; and sometimes I pray.

Just the other day, I went back to my 1976 daybook to check on the date of my father's death. While thumbing through the pages, I happened to see the entry I wrote after hearing our beloved pastor, Robert Fine, preach his last sermon before succumbing to colon cancer. His image came back to me: I saw him leaning against the pulpit and heard him hoarsely whisper the prayer of François Fénelon: "Smite me, or heal me, depress me, or raise me up....I adore all thy purposes, without knowing them."[13]

Once again, I claimed the prayer for my own. It stands out like a jewel in the collection of my days.

In retirement I am still keeping my daybook, but the content is changing. Without a heavy schedule of appointments, I pay greater attention to the emotions I feel and the insights I gain.

Recently, I decided I would record lessons that I learned each day. Starting off the day open to new learning, and closing the day with a moment's reflection on what I have learned, I feel amazed at the result. I see myself reaching out in human experience and going deeper in spiritual understanding than ever before. Without the clutter of the daily grind, more room opens up for breadth in human experience and depth in spiritual understanding.

Even now, I envision an entry in the daybook on the last day of my life. It will be the lesson learned on that day and proof that we can learn as long as we live.

PART **IV**

Laugh at Yourself

15

Why Do I Now Read the Obituaries Ahead of *Peanuts*?

Do you remember the old man who opened his newspaper to the obituaries each morning to see if his name appeared there? If it didn't, he got up and went about his business.

Age has a way of changing our reading habits. My lifelong pattern for going through the newspaper used to follow a specific sequence: front page news, sports, *Peanuts*, editorials, and then business. With only a glance and shudder, I avoided the obituary page. Unless a person of prominence had died and deserved a picture, I never read the details of death. And even in those cases, I skimmed the words to prevent any ghoulish fixation.

Confessing My Fear

A psychoanalyst would love to hear how I developed my aversion to death. Right off, I would admit that my actions came from a subconscious fear of death. As a counseling psychologist myself, I also know that the therapist would interpret my fear as reaction formation against a death wish deep within me. My story would then unfold.

At an early age, I heard hellfire sermons that caused me to see my sinful soul snapping and popping in the flames. Like the members of Jonathan Edwards's congregation who heard his sermon "Sinners in the Hands of an Angry God" my knuckles would turn white as I gripped the pew ahead of me in order to keep from falling into hell.

My camp meeting background is not solely to blame. Junior high literature classes reinforced my fear of death. Although we had to read Shakespeare and other classics, weird bits of poetry still stick in my mind. From memory, I can quote from Edgar Allan Poe's "The Raven," a symbol of guilt and death: "Take thy beak from out my heart, and take thy form from off my door!"

Or from William Cullen Bryant's "Thanatopsis":

By an unfaltering trust, approach thy grave,
Like one who wraps the drapery of this couch
About him, and lies down to pleasant dreams.

And from Percy Bysshe Shelley's "Ozymandias of Egypt," I particularly remember what it says is written on Ozymandias's toppled monument in the desert:

"My name is Ozymandias, king of kings:
Look on my works, ye mighty and despair!"
Nothing beside remains: round the decay
Of that colossal wreck, boundless and bare,
The lone and level sands stretch far away.

Death is the common theme, guilt the common thread, and futility the common end. Although I am an optimist about life, and suicide has never crossed my mind, the psychoanalyst would most likely find the fear of death lurking beneath the surface. My Christian faith has helped a bit, but when I thought about writing a book on the promise of the resurrection—"O death, where is thy sting? O grave, where is thy victory?"—I came up with the tentative title *The Sting of Victory*.

The psychoanalyst probably would prescribe shock treatment.

Discovering God's Gift

There is more to my story. Something has happened to change the way I read the newspaper. The turning point may have come from Henri Nouwen's book *Our Greatest Gift*.

Among the many spiritual insights in the book, one stands out. Nouwen reminds us that we are one with the human family at least two times in our life. Once: at the moment of birth, when we are totally helpless and dependent upon others. The other: at the moment of death, when we are again totally helpless and dependent upon others. Nouwen writes of the grace hidden in our powerlessness: "The great gift hidden in our dying is the gift of unity with all people."[14] More than that, we become parents of generations to come. This is why Nouwen can write, "The fruitfulness of our lives shows itself in its fullness only after we have died."[15] Rather than coming to the futility of Thanatopsis or the obliteration of Ozymandias, Nouwen sees these moments as the time when all humans are equally one as children of God.

To stand equal in the presence of God is not our dread; it is our hope. Coming to that moment, trusting in the resurrected Christ as our Savior, is our glorious hope. From the perspective of faith, death loses its sting and the grave is robbed of its victory.

Learning from a Fable

Nouwen puts all of these thoughts together in a memorable little fable. Let me repeat it in abbreviated form.

Twins are talking to each other in the womb. The sister says to the brother, "I believe there is life after birth."

Her brother says, "No, this is all there is."

But the sister answers, "There must be something more than this dark place." Momentarily, the sister remains quiet, but then makes the daring statement, "I think there is a mother out there."

The brother explodes, "*What* are you talking about? I have never seen a mother, and neither have you."

His words silence his sister once again. Finally, she screws up her courage and asks, "Don't you feel these squeezes once in a while? They are very unpleasant and sometimes painful."

Skepticism colors the brother's response: "What's so special about that?"

His undaunted sister speaks with hope: "Well, I think that these squeezes are there to get us ready for another place, much more beautiful than this, where we will see our mother face-to-face. Don't you think that is exciting?"

Call me sentimental if you will, but Nouwen's fable taught me what it means to live and die well. As witness to my new-found understanding, I can read the obituaries ahead of *Peanuts*. I haven't gone so far as some of my friends, who have written their own obituaries, composed their own epitaphs, and planned their own funeral services. That may come. But for now I am wonderfully content with the knowledge that death is an extension of our life, grace is a gift of our powerlessness, and the forgiveness of Christ is our hope for eternal life.

16

Will My Mansion Have a Doghouse?

Even bad jokes can raise good questions. A man had to put his beloved dog to sleep after many years of companionship. In his grief, he went to see an Episcopalian priest with the question, "Will you conduct a funeral for my dog?"

The priest answered, "Oh, no, we have no liturgy for the funeral of a dog."

Trying again, the man went to a Baptist pastor with the same question. He got a similar answer: "Oh, no, our theology doesn't include dogs."

Undeterred, the man tried again, this time with a Methodist minister. Again, he got the answer, "Oh, no, our Book of Discipline doesn't cover the death of dogs."

With slumped shoulders, the man turned away. But then, understanding what might be wrong, he looked back at the Methodist minister and asked, "Do you think a $500 honorarium is too little to ask a minister to bury a dog?"

The question struck fire in the eyes of the minister, who exclaimed, "Oh, I am sorry. You didn't tell me your dog was a Methodist!"

A Theological Twist

We laugh because the story seems so ludicrous, but then we wonder about the question.

For me, there was no doubt. Dogs have no immortal souls and therefore no place in heaven. This was my unquestioned stance until I learned that my two most trusted theological mentors both believed otherwise. C. S. Lewis, in his book *The Problem of Pain*, argues that we need our pets with us in heaven if we are to be complete.[16] Then I learned that the founding father of my Wesleyan tradition also believed that animals would be part of the great redemption when animal, vegetable, and mineral will be restored to their pristine state in the new creation. Believe it or not, John Wesley not only contended for the salvation of animals, but even proposed that "God would move the various animals higher up the Chain of Being in the next life—granting them greater abilities, including perhaps even the ability to relate to God as humans do now!"[17]

Moments ago, I held Molly, our Maltese, up to a mirror to see if she would recognize her image or bark at the doggie in the glass. Her total lack of response reminded me that self-awareness is evidence of God's image in us, and a critical distinction between animals and human beings. If Wesley is right, is it possible that God's gift in heaven to the lower order of creation will be self-awareness? With self-awareness, however, Molly would gain memory, reflection, humor, conscience, guilt, awe, and reverence.

In other words, she would be human.

At first, my theological mentors disappointed me. How could such intelligent men as C. S. Lewis and John Wesley believe that animals will be in heaven and possibly be elevated to a higher level of existence?

Now, however, I am not so sure. Let me tell you the story.

Poochie and the Linebacker

When I was president of Asbury Theological Seminary, our vice-president for finance was Eugene Lintemuth. In his youth, he starred as a high school linebacker in football and later excelled as a leading salesman for John Deere tractors. He was a formidable figure with a no-nonsense approach to finances.

As my vice president at Asbury, I could turn any project over to him and trust him implicitly. Like a bulldog, he carried the overload of balancing the budget, nursing the endowment, and rebuilding the campus—until he had a heart attack that required five bypasses. As he recovered, he learned that little dogs have a therapeutic effect upon heart patients. So he and his wife bought a little black poodle named Poochie.

And then the ludicrous took over.

Gene and Poochie became inseparable friends, sleeping together, walking together, and, whenever possible, shopping together. For their retirement travels back and forth to Michigan and Florida, the Lintemuths bought an RV that could also be home for Poochie. Of course, we all laughed at the sight of a seventy-year-old, former linebacker, cuddling a tiny black poodle in his arms.

Molly and the President

My chuckle at Gene Lintemuth's expense turned into a gulp. Three years into my retirement, I, too, became a member of what we call "The Zipper Club." Only those who have the scar down the front of their chest need apply. The scar is our badge of honor as survivors of bypass heart surgery. I joined the club after a triple bypass in 1997.

Three years later, the kids decided that Mom needed a dog. So on Christmas morning they brought out a large box wrapped in festive foil for her to open. When she lifted the lid, out popped a little white fuzzy ball of a Maltese puppy. At first, Jan thought she did not want to keep the dog because it would become a problem when we wanted to travel. Within the first week, I had a buyer ready to take the dog off our hands. But Jan weighed the decision and said, "No, I love her." So, according to her registry at the American Kennel Club, "Miss Molly McKenna" became our dog.

Or — should I confess — *my* dog.

Molly cried the first night we had her, so I brought her into bed with me, where she cuddled in the crook of my arm. Guess where she sleeps now? At naptimes and bedtimes, Molly is in the crook of my arm. After breathing a big sigh, she settles down to sleep as long as Jan and I sleep.

For a guy who vowed that no dog would ever sleep in his bed, I became a wimp because of Molly. She is my dog. When I rise, she waits for me to take her out. When I write, she curls on the pillow under my desk. When I walk, she scurries out in front of me. When I stay away too long, she scolds me. When evening comes and she needs to go out, she gives an authoritative command. We never took Molly to obedience school, but she schooled us. Her daily routine makes her a perfect dog.

Before retirement, a dog in the house was a chore; after retirement and heart surgery, Molly is the one who calms me down by a look of confidence in her eyes, lifts me up with a wag of the tail when I come home, and gives me hope as she responds to such simple questions as, "Molly want a treat?" "Molly want dinner?" or "Molly want to go bye-bye?" No longer am I — a former college, university, and seminary president — ashamed to appear in public with a little white Maltese in my arms. Molly has become my Poochie.

The funniest picture I can imagine would be David McKenna, the tough chief executive, and Eugene Lintemuth, his trusted chief financial officer, posing together for a retirement photograph with little white Molly and little black Poochie in their arms. All other contradictions would cease. We are at the command of our dogs.

So the profound theological question remains: "Will my mansion have a doghouse?" I think I know the answer.

The theology of Molly begins with the fact that a dog is God's handiwork—a victim of human sin, but incapable of sinning, and yet groaning as she waits for the final redemption of all creation. Meanwhile, Molly trusts me implicitly, loves me unconditionally, forgives me whenever I leave her, begs for forgiveness when she is bad, watches my feet for a sense of direction, thrives under the watchful eye of God, and always looks up with a hopeful eye.

And so all doubt is erased. If animals go to heaven, then Molly will be there.

Now it is up to me to make sure that *I* have a mansion to go with the doghouse.

17

How Soon Do You Need to Know?

Our retirement began in the senior community of Sun City, Nevada. To qualify for residence, at least one member of the family has to be fifty-five years or older. Children under the age of nineteen are not allowed to live there, and visits of grandchildren are limited to a maximum of six months. These policies shape the culture of the community.

Golf, bridge, square dancing, crafts, water aerobics, lawn bowling, and gambling dominate the interests of the citizens. A little tennis and handball adds piquancy to the climate. But give the seniors credit. We all roar at old-age jokes, topped by this one: An old man sits on a bench in a park at Sun City. Another old man comes up and sits next to him. At first, they do not speak. Then, one old man slowly turns his head toward the other and asks, "Hi. What's your name?" His bench partner looks back with a blank stare and pauses for a long minute before answering, "How soon do you need to know?"

Two Heads are Better than One

Jokes about the declining memory of senior citizens frighten us because they are so true. Even the most active minds begin to lose details of the moment while retaining specifics of the past.

My wife and I laugh together when we try to remember the names of old friends. The quip, "I'll never forget what's-her-name" gets heard more and more often as we age. My approach to the loss of a friend's name is to mentally go through the alphabet, with hope that the name will pop up. Sometimes it does; often it doesn't. So we laugh again and say, "Two heads are better than one." Going deep into thought, we think and think until one of us says, "I am sure that her name begins with an *S*." The cue starts the wheels turning until one of us has a flash of recognition and announces, "Susie! Her first name is Susie." The other then adds, "Right. It is Susie Oaks." High fives celebrate our mental triumph.

With advancing age, two heads are definitely better than one.

When the Mask Comes Off

We joke about what we fear. My wife's two parents lived into their nineties, on two very different paths.

As I wrote earlier (I didn't forget!), her father began to show signs of senility in his late seventies when the doctor discovered a clogging of the carotid artery. After surgery, his mind cleared, but his body continued to age. The difference was more than he could handle, and resentment over aging got translated into disgruntlement that carried over into his interpersonal relationships, especially with his wife. Fussiness with detail, control over minor items, and dissatisfaction with results turned one of the happiest of men into a conundrum.

Not too many years after his surgery, my wife's mom began to show serious signs of senility. The symptoms advanced rapidly and turned the saintliest of women into a person with unexpected reactions that ranged from hostility to humor. For the first time, she struck out at me because I had "sold her home and put her in nursing care." As a pastor's wife for forty-four years, church services were her life. But when the staff of the nursing center invited her to a chapel service, she slashed a finger across her throat and snapped, "I've had it UP TO HERE with church!" Later, when her husband broke his back and was confined to bed, the medical staff let Mom stay in the same room with him. That is, until she yanked him out of bed and onto the floor, saying, "Get up. It's time to go to work."

Glimpses of Eternity

If we live long enough, most of us will lose touch with reality and forget the names of those we love. In one sense, it is a merciful antidote for the emotional pain of aging. But in another sense, it is a tragic loss of personhood.

On the way to that loss, memory of the past comes sharp and clear while memory of the present disappears from moment to moment. As that happens to us, we have a special gift to give to our children as we connect them with family history and events that would be lost forever, except for the mystery of memory. It is also the time when we cash in on the capital of love and trust that has been building through the years.

Even as the mind gets fogged, senility is not complete. Some of the most miraculous stories come from those moments. In the case of my wife's mother, we debated whether to take her to the funeral service of her only son. She sat through the service without any sign of recognition, but when we escorted her to the casket, she looked into the face of her son and asked, "Is my son in heaven?"

Alzheimer's is the disease we dread most. For a married couple, there are always two victims, the person with the disease and the spouse who survives. And the disease plays no favorites. Nancy Reagan suffered immeasurably when her husband no longer recognized her and required twenty-four-hour care. She deserves our tribute, as do so many other spouses who have gone through similar dark days.

I often tell the story of Robertson McQuilken, a presidential colleague, whose wife developed Alzheimer's at the peak of his career. All of us remember Muriel, because Robertson brought her to our annual meeting for seminary presidents and spouses, hoping that the fellowship might give her a spark of recognition. At the last meeting they attended, Muriel slipped in and out of awareness. Finally, with recognition almost gone, McQuillken resigned from the presidency in order to care for his wife. In one of the most poignant letters ever written, he writes, "If I took care of her for forty years, I would never be out of her debt."

As he read article after article on Alzheimer's, he kept reading that the real victim of the disease is not the patient, but the caregiver. Colleagues probably had that thought in mind when they urged him to put Muriel in a care facility and get on with his life. Robertson disputed any idea that he was a victim by answering, "I don't *have* to care for her. I *get* to."

Few of us will be as eloquent as Robertson McQuilken, but any of us can demonstrate the depth of our relationship with our loved ones. My only sister, Pat, had a major stroke some years ago. A brilliant professor holding a Ph.D. from the University of Michigan; a well-known author in the field of business education; a pioneer in founding her local Presbyterian church and revitalizing civic leadership for the Salvation Army; and a fast-walking, fun-loving member of her senior community; she was left to type with one finger, one good leg, a faulty heart valve, and endless physical complications that required constant medical care. Her faith in God is the antidote to depression, while her love of life is the remedy for despair.

But the other side of the story is the love of her husband and caregiver, Jim.

By nature, Jim is an impatient person who can fire on a short fuse and let incompetent people feel his displeasure. Only his love for Pat could transform him into a caregiver, unbelieveably patient in the long haul of limited rehabilitation, physical breakdown, emotional stress, and mental confusion. He has his moments, of course, and more than once we have heard the report, "We could have killed each other last night." In those times, love that is "patient, long-suffering, and kind" is greater than the frustration and despair of the moment. In his own way, Jim is acting out the words of Robertson McQuilken: "I don't *have* to care for her. I *get* to."

In the Image of God

Does it seem like a long way between a joke about forgetting names to the grim reality of senility, Alzheimer's, and a major stroke? In truth, the distance is not so far as we might think.

As we grow old physically, we also grow old mentally. Does this mean that the image of God gets blurred in us? Is our humanity demeaned? Is our personhood diminished? Not at all. In fact, mental aging *doubles* the meaning of God's image in us.

One side of his image is seen in how we respond to aging. We need not become mean, humorless, and disgruntled victims of mental decline. As witness to our faith, we can be young in spirit, laugh at our foibles, and relish every moment of life.

The other side of his image is the way in which we respond to our personal relationships. In dotage, we need not become lonely isolates. As a continuing expression of their love, our spouses and our children become companions on the journey. When we are forgetful, they laugh with us; when our mental functions slip, they compensate for us; and if our memories are lost, they care for us.

18

What Else Can I Do
While I'm Down Here?

When I first heard the quip from an arthritic friend, "What else can I do while I'm down here?" I laughed and laughed. Think of an old guy with stiff joints and a sore back, bending over to pick up something from the floor. As the bones creak and the back rebels, he knows that he will not be doing this again except in emergencies. So, he asks himself, "What else can I do while I'm down here?"

I laugh no more. Not too many years ago, I stretched daily with arms swinging from toe to toe and then followed with five minutes of sit-ups. Now, when I make effort to pick up something from the floor, I too, ask, "What else can I do while I'm down here?"

This question involves more than an aching body. As we grow older, we have to learn the economics of aging. Ordinarily, we bend over to pick up something and then do it again as needed. No more. By looking around and seeing something else to do, we conserve our energy and increase our efficiency.

Sooner or later, we apply this lesson to every area of life. Without energy to waste or inefficiency to burn, we learn to put tasks together and make priority decisions.

Changing Worlds

One reality of retirement is that we are not simply going through a change in the life cycle; in fact, we are in transition between worlds. Change is a step forward, backward, or sideways along a given path (such as changing jobs); but *transition* is a transformation in the way we look at the world and how we see ourselves.

In other words, change is positional while transition is personal.

After change, we are the same person in a different position; but after transition, we are a different person in a different position. Retirement is not change; it is transition. Just like the old man bending down to pick up something from the floor, the outlook is different and his self-perception is different.

How do we adjust to the transition called retirement? My answer is this: If the cardinal rule for purchasing real estate is "Location, location, location," then the counterpart for the transition into retirement is "Simplify, simplify, simplify." The process begins with what William Bridges, a guru of life transitions, calls "old endings."

Most of us will admit that we come to retirement with a cluttered and complicated life. In contemporary parlance, this is called "baggage." Before we can go forward into the "new beginnings" that retirement promises us, we have to decide on the baggage that we will leave behind.

Tagging Baggage

In his book *The Way of Transition*, Bridges tells of a company that specialized in relocating corporate employees overseas. It suggested the use of four distinct stickers to correctly direct the movers:[18]

> AIR—To be used for the important items that you need immediately at the new location

> SEA—To be used for items that you want to take along, but that are not so important as to require fast transit

> STORAGE—To be used for items that you don't want to discard, but that you also know you really don't want to use just now

> STAY—To be used for items that you realize you need to get rid of and leave behind

To put this discipline to test on the baggage we bring into retirement is no idle exercise. We quickly learn what we need and what we don't need. It puts legs under the first rule of retirement, "Simplify, simplify, simplify."

Clearing the Clutter

When I look back upon the ten years of my retirement, I see how I used these stickers in moving from a change in position to a transition in person. While we can make a quick change in position when we enter retirement, it can take years to make the transition as a person. At least, that is the way it was for me. Going from change to transition involved two major steps.

For our first step, we planned to locate in Seattle, Washington, where we had a very small retirement home that needed renovation and the addition of an upper story. When the cost proved prohibitive, we began to look at other options. Although I had not yet read Bridges's book, I realize now that I was sorting out personal values in preparation for change. If a moving company had written a bill of lading for our baggage, it might have looked like this:

AIR — A new, one-story home; a warm climate; and proximity to family

SEA — A local church, friends, inspiration for writing, and health care

STORAGE — Speaking, consulting, board memberships, and future earnings

STAY — Any thought of locating in the community from which we retired, returning to the Midwest, accepting another presidency, or retaining any formal position in the institution from which we retired

With these stickers guiding our change into retirement, we sold the Seattle house and bought a new, one-story home in Sun City, situated on a golf course and around the corner from my only sister and her husband. With the priority items that came by "air" in place, we began unpacking the items labeled "sea" and started asking questions about the things still in "storage."

Five fast years went by as our introduction to retirement. We enjoyed all of the benefits of a new home, a warm climate, a close relationship with my sister, and frequent golf games with my brother-in-law. During this time, my sister had a stroke and we were so grateful to be present to support her during recovery and rehabilitation.

For some reason, we never found a church home in Sun City and we made few new friends. Years in the presidency and transcontinental moves made Jan and me self-contained as a couple, and put our focus on our children and grandchildren. Writing became more important to me as I set the goal of completing a book a year — the schedule interrupted by triple bypass surgery after three years in Sun City.

During this time, I continued speak and consult occasionally and attend a limited number of board meetings. Never once did we second-guess our decision to retire by wanting to retrieve the "stay" items that we had left behind. The transition was almost complete.

We had moved beyond our past position into the status called "retirement."

19

Why Are My Major Symptoms Called 'Side-Effects'?

If good humor is a sense of the ludicrous, then the funniest sketches on television are not in sitcoms, comedies, home videos, or bloopers. Hilarity is *actually* found in the commercials that advertise drugs for everything from satisfying sex to eliminating heartburn, preventing pregnancy, and healing herpes.

If you want a good laugh, listen carefully to their promises.

Elderly Elixirs

Senior citizens are a prime target for drugs that revive sex, eliminate wrinkles, cure incontinence, improve memory, fight depression, and boost energy. Smiling, beautiful, and air-brushed faces appear on the screen to convince us that the drugs will work the miracle of an extreme makeover.

There is no doubt about it. Pharmaceutical companies want us to rush to our doctor and demand that he or she prescribe their product. Only Food and Drug Administration laws force them to add footnotes in fine print, warning us about side effects that can do far more damage than the drug can do good.

In most cases, the chances of serious side effects are limited to a small percentage of users. Still, anyone who reads the fine print will wonder about the risk of such common symptoms as nausea, vomiting, dizziness, chest pain, headaches, weakness, high blood pressure, liver damage, and diarrhea. Even if you have only a small chance of having any one of these symptoms, the accumulative effect makes you ask, "Is it really worth it?"

Here is where a sense of humor checks in:

Stealth Symptoms: A drug touted to treat migraine headaches is followed by a long list of negatives, but then "balanced" by the encouraging words, "This is not a complete list of side effects."

Male Pregnancy: A drug to restore hair on balding men begins with the warning, "Do not use if you are a woman," and then, after a listing of symptoms (including itchy scalp, patches of hair growth, and reddening of the skin), is another warning: "Do not use if you are pregnant or breast feeding."

Psychological Snake Oil: A mood-enhancing drug carries the warning, "Do not take if you are bipolar (manic depressive)."

Catch 22: A birth-control injection given four times a year takes away the nuisance of pills and patches, but increases the chance of bone fractures due to loss of bone strength and results in weight gain for two out of three users.

User-unfriendly: A drug to reduce acid reflux notes that no difference is found in the safety of elderly and younger people who take the drug, but "greater sensitivity of some older people cannot be ruled out."

These tidbits of humor make us choke while we chuckle, and they explain why drug companies have to buy two pages in a magazine to sell their products. The front page touts the drug in glossy, four-color pictures of beautiful people, while the back page posts the research report, along with all of the possible side effects (in type so small you need a magnifying glass to read it). Of course, that is the point of fine print. The drug company doesn't want you to read it. If you do, you either will not take the drug, or live in fear of the nasty consequences.

Beware of BSPI

The fine print of drug ads usually gets introduced by the high-sounding title, "Brief Summary of Prescribing Information," or euphemistically translated BSPI. True to savvy sales strategy, the fine print begins with one sentence usually called "Indications," which touts the benefit of the drug.

And then begins the march of negatives.

Before your eyes, you see the titles of "Contraindications," "Warnings," "Precautions," "Adverse Reactions," and "Overdosage." The list seems so long and threatening that the reader comes away feeling as if taking the medication amounts to a "crapshoot" on one's life. You also come to understand why doctors talk about the "practice" of medicine and we are given the name "patient"! It is a good thing that doctors take the Hippocratic oath. When it comes to drugs, we have to put our lives in the hands of healthcare professionals.

Before retirement, I took only two drugs: one for cholesterol and one for acid reflux. Now, after heart surgery, I am a walking pillbox. In addition to the drugs for cholesterol and acid reflux, I have pills for reducing the workload of the heart, lowering high blood pressure, combating dry mouth, and — in case of angina — a blast of nitroglycerine. To supplement these prescriptions, I have vitamins for old age and prevention of memory loss, drops for dry eyes, and baby aspirin as the catch-all and cure-all.

Do I experience side effects? You bet.

Despite a maintenance diet and daily exercise, I fight the "body bloat" or "weight gain" cited as side effects on three of my pills. No one knows for sure whether my daily fatigue is old age or the draining effect of too many pills. A recent increase in the drugs to reduce my total cholesterol and its bad LDL must have sent the wrong signal to my large intestine, because the food that goes into my mouth does not stop on the way out. When the doctor checked on the drugs I was taking for the side effect of diarrhea, he returned from his office with a wry smile on his face and said, "At least three of them could cause this problem."

To add to the drama (and the dilemma), a routine check of my pulse revealed the new symptom of an irregular heartbeat. What is the doctor's remedy? "Stop drinking Starbucks coffee." Now, to prescribe such a draconian cure for a Seattleite is like asking me to stop living. More than that, the doctor's advice created a spiritual crisis for me. I could relate to George Buttrick, the great American preacher, when he was asked by a parishioner if he kept the "morning watch." Buttrick answered, "Lady, until I have a cup of coffee, I am an atheist."

So, on I go, popping pills, drinking Starbucks, staying close to the bathroom, and ignoring the doctor's advice.

The Solitary Lesson

The only lesson I can learn from the brutal reality called "aging" is that the human body is so finely tuned that the slightest change in its chemistry can upset the whole system. Along with our doctors, we must dedicate ourselves to doing what we can to maintain that fine balance.

It is the difference between the wholeness of health and the breakdown of illness. Even at our best, when it comes to drugs, we are like gamblers playing the odds. We have to go with the percentages, trust our doctor, and pray that the statistics do not catch up with us.

PART V

Grow Down

20

What's So Great about Grandma's House?

Among the best of my childhood memories is going to Grandma's house for Thanksgiving or Christmas and hearing Dad sing,

Over the river and through the woods,
To grandmother's house we go.
The horse knows the way,
To carry the sleigh,
Through white and drifted snow.

Michigan winters often provided the setting for the song. But the real romance came at the moment my sister and I exploded through the door of Grandma's house, caught the smell of turkey in the oven, wrapped ourselves in her arms, and felt her kiss upon our cheeks.

Years later, I am asking myself, "What's so great about Grandma's house?" Is it the place where we felt our roots? Is it remembered as the center of a special love? Is it the memory of family get-togethers?

The answer to all of these questions is yes...but there is more.

Another image comes into view. When our parents' marriage fell apart and we lived in a house filled either with shouts or silence, my sister and I found refuge in Grandma's house. Sister remembers fleeing the hostility of a fractured home, running up the street, falling into Grandma's arms, and crying, "Hold me." I remember telling Grandma my plight after I led my first song service in church. Thinking that all good song leaders say something between their selections, I chose to introduce "Amazing Grace" by saying that although John Newton discovered the law of gravity when an apple fell on his head, his greater discovery was the amazing grace of God. As gently as possible, Grandma told me, "It was Isaac Newton, not John Newton, who discovered the law of gravity. But don't worry, I didn't see anyone who knew the difference."

Because my wife and I lived in a president's home on or near a college, university, or seminary campus for thirty-three consecutive years, our children and grandchildren never had a place that they could truly call "home." So when it came to the time of retirement, we wanted a place that the kids *could* call "home" and the grandkids could remember as "Grandma's house." But it didn't happen all at once.

A Golf Course and a Guest Room

Talk about a change of worlds! Upon retirement we moved from Wilmore, Kentucky—a peaceful village whose two stoplights turn to blinkers at ten o'clock at night—across the country to Las Vegas, Nevada, a 24/7 city kept awake by millions of neon lights. Word rippled across the country and through the ranks of our Christian friends, "The McKennas have moved to *Sin City*!"

It takes too long to explain that the Lord led us there. But I can justify our decision: After more than three decades in president's homes on or near the campuses we served, we wanted a new home, on one floor, near family (my only sister lives in Las Vegas), and in a place where it is warm.

We got our choice. Even though the standing joke was that Sun City homes were built of "toothpicks, mud, and spit," we thoroughly enjoyed a 2,180-square-foot home on the fifth green of the golf course. Try as we might to change our mailing address to Summerlin, Nevada, it invariably came back as Las Vegas.

We had an eventful five years in that home. As I said, when my sister had a major stroke, we knew why God had led us to be there during the crisis. I also developed heart disease that required triple bypass surgery.

Contrary to the stereotype, residents of Las Vegas do not have to be gamblers, buffet gourmets, or showtime buffs. Nearby Summerlin, for instance, is an upscale community with strong evangelical churches and refined cultural opportunities. And from our retirement base in Nevada, we could quickly fly to Michigan, Washington, Ohio, or California, where our four children lived. We planned to have the children visit us at least once a year, and we would return a visit to them. Of course, there was also an understanding that we would do everything within our power to be present for the birth or graduation of grandchild.

But our best-laid plans went awry when our two younger children found a way to return to Seattle. Suzanne got a job transfer with Lenscrafters and Rob took a teaching position at Seattle Pacific University.

Then it happened.

Shortly after Suzanne, Scott, and their three boys moved back to Seattle, our five-year-old grandson, Sean, came home from school and asked, "Mommy, why can't I stop at Grandma's house for cookies like the other kids?" That was all Grandma needed. Within days, a "For Sale" sign sprouted on our front lawn.

A Garden and a Bonus Room

Once we knew that we were leaving Las Vegas, we looked at many options in Seattle—both condos and homes. Then we got the message. Our oldest son, Doug, had seen a model home on the Issaquah plateau, east of Seattle, in a place called Sammamish that prompted him to say, "Sell the farm and buy this one."

When we visited the home, we were awed. It stood on a corner lot as the feature for a new development of homes in "Timberline Ridge." If any home ever met the real estate standards of "location, location, location," this was it. Furthermore, it met our requirements of a master bedroom on the first level (for folks growing old), a study with a fireplace for my writing, an island in the kitchen for Jan's cooking, a garden with colors for every season, and a patio for my barbecue grill.

The builder had given his imagination free rein both inside and outside the house. It had "curb appeal" in the front that brought bidders to the door. Spirits soared as one stepped into the foyer and saw the cathedral ceilings. Nothing could be better—except its size and price; in those areas we were over our heads. Size took care of itself, however, as we thought about entertaining the family with plenty of running room. My wife and I each have memories of "Grandma's house" that we wanted to pass on to our children and grandchildren.

When we inquired about purchasing the home, we found that buyers were standing in line. But since it was a model, the contractor had refused to sell it—until we came along. When we met with the contractor's agent, *something* happened. She knew and we knew that this was to be our home. So we made a quick decision. Rather than having a second home—a house in the sun, a cottage on a lake, or an RV for a cross-country trip—we would stretch our investment into one place called "Grandma's house."

Our next surprise came when our contingency offer on the Sammamish home was met by a Las Vegas buyer. A man walked into our Sun City home, looked around, and said, "I want to buy your home just as it is—with all of the furniture, pictures, and accessories." Three weeks later, Janet and I turned the key in the front door after a moving van picked up our clothing, my books and the family memorabilia. Talk about fun!

Imagine starting over with a fund for decorating a new home that already had a head start as the builder's model. But with that we learned what beleaguered homeowners mean when they say, "We have wall-to-wall carpeting and back-to-the-wall payments." Nevertheless, by staying with the discipline of investing in one home and conserving on other expenditures, five years later, we burned the mortgage.

Our bigger and better retirement home quickly became the gathering place for after-school stopovers, Sunday night pizza, and dinners celebrating holidays, birthdays, and anniversaries. Grandkids came to the front door, took off their shoes, and ran upstairs to watch television and eat the snacks that Grandma had ready for them. For almost six years, Grandma's house got better every day.

A View and Dining Space

One day, after five years in Seattle, Jan and I sat in our mom and pop chairs—where we drink coffee, read the paper, have devotions, and make plans for the day—and our conversation turned into a short course in "elderly economics." An offer had come to buy a one-bedroom condo in Palm Desert, California.

For years we had toyed with the idea, but when we took a pencil to the expenses, it always came out as a deficit. Now in retirement with no debt on our Sammamish home, we could go south with so many of our friends to escape the rainy winters and enjoy the little condo. Here is where the three principles of elderly economics checked in. We decided that it was time to:

Simplify our life,

Downsize our home, and

Outsource our maintenance.

You can read between the lines of these working principles. We got tired just thinking about the obligations of a second home—whether a condo in Palm Desert or an RV on the road. The reality of two people rambling around in a big house no longer made sense. Most of all, we could no longer keep up with home, lawn, and garden maintenance. We knew that within five years, we would be forced to make a move. So, putting elderly economics into practice, we began a year-long discussion of our options.

Starting with retirement centers, we put one deposit on an urban high-rise and another on a rural duplex. Our strong sense of independence caused us to struggle as we considered living on a schedule that included two meals a day, shared with senior citizens wall-to-wall. For many people, these arrangements feel ideal. But they reminded Janet of the camp meetings in her childhood—and I had the feeling we were going back to the years of eating in the dining commons of the institutions where we served. So we hedged our bets by keeping the deposit on one of the two—the urban high-rise assisted-living unit—just in case one of us became incapacitated and we needed care. Then we searched for a simpler and smaller home that would also meet our dreams of a Western view on the waterfront.

Condos in Kirkland, Washington—bordering Lake Washington and looking west to the Olympic Mountains—became our target area. But the shock of reality hit us again. Real estate prices in Seattle were escalating at a rate competitive with that of the Southern California coast. We soon learned that we would have to hike up our budget in order to downsize our home. But by taking advantage of the appreciation on our Sammamish home and putting the second home money into a single unit, we decided that we could go for broke.

Over a period of months, two condos came into view. We made an offer on one but lost to a bidder who blew the fuses on the purchase price. Our second offer was better, but the owners took one look at their options and decided to stay put. Throughout this process, we prayed, "Lord, don't let us make a mistake." In retrospect, we realize that the first offer would have been a mistake and the second offer was turned down because God had something better. We settled back into the position to stay put in our Sammamish home for another five years, after which we planned to move into the retirement center.

Then one afternoon, our real estate agent called to say that a condo in Kirkland on the waterfront had just come up online. "Would you like to see it?" he asked. By now we felt skeptical about finding a place that we could afford, but we decided it never hurt to look.

As we walked into the condo, Jan headed toward the master bedroom and I took a look at the study. We met in the kitchen a minute or two later and Jan said, "Let's buy it."

Within one hour, we had a full-price offer on the table.

The timing was uncanny. Within minutes, two other buyers made offers above the asking price, indicating they were ready for a bidding war. The listing agent, however, fell in love with our grandson and our family. At the risk of making other bidders angry, she took our offer to the sellers and they immediately agreed.

Our emotions in the next three months careened up and down like a ride on a roller coaster. Everyone said that our Sammamish home would sell in the first week. They were still saying the same thing two months later. Either the price was too high, there were not enough bedrooms, a corner lot was a disadvantage, the house wasn't "kid-friendly," or the garden was too big. As a self-confessed control freak, I felt greater stress than I knew in all my years as a chief executive in higher education. Both my wife and I realized that stress was taking its toll on us. In fact, after the house finally sold and the movers came, I had an angina attack. While the nitroglycerine took effect, the kids arrived to supervise the move.

To say that miracles countered the stress may sound flippant, but for us it is the only term that applies. A 2 percent loan carried us through the period when we owned two homes at the same time. The inspection of the condo revealed the necessity of three fix-its, but they cost only $20 each. When a second inspection of the stucco on the Sammamish house added to our stress, it, too, came back with three problems that I could resolve in minutes. Best of all, every piece of furniture fit the new condo like a glove.

Now, each evening Jan and I sit at our bedroom window, enjoying the view overlooking a park and Lake Washington. Even in the rainy days that typify Seattle, we see glorious sunsets against the Olympic Mountains and remember the final words of the listing agent who sold us the condo: "God had a hand in this."

One sober lesson follows this story. We now realize how much the stress of buying and selling took its toll on us. If a few more years were added and we were in our later seventies, we know that someone else would have had to make the move for us.

Jesus' words to Peter are so true. In the final chapter of the Gospel of John, the Master says, "I tell you the truth, when you were younger you dressed yourself and went where you wanted; but when you are old you will stretch our your hands, and someone else will dress you and lead you where you do not want to go" (John 21:18).

Just such a time is coming for all of us blessed with long life. But being forced to move from our home into a retirement center is not one of the decisions that I want to defer. Bruce Barton, the advertising executive, said in the *New York Times*, "When you are through changing, you are through."

I want to keep changing as long as I can, and within the will of God, I want to control that change.

A chuckle wraps up the story. Our two youngest children contributed to pushing us to leave the large Sammamish home and buy a condo. Even though they had fond memories of all the pizza parties and holiday dinners at Grandma's house, they went online daily to see if they could find a condo for us. Each time we viewed a place, they were there before us. When we went to look at the condo we finally bought, they brought their whole family. Not until the deal was done did they tip their hand. With a knowing smile on her face, Suzanne observed, "One of the best things about your new condo is the dining room. You actually have more space to add leaves to the table than you did before."

My wife answered, "I thought that one of the reasons for downsizing was to have the children take turns hosting family dinners."

Ha! Not long after we moved in, we got the phone call: "Mom, your grandchildren want to have Easter dinner in your new condo. Don't worry. We'll bring the food." What could Jan say? She overworked herself getting the place ready, and she went out of her way to make sure she had the grandchildren's favorite appetizers and side dishes. All I had to do was put the leaves in the dining room table, sweep the deck, and slice the ham.

It was an occasion to be remembered, and not only for the family meal, and the strong sense of the theme, "Christ the Lord is risen today. Alleluia!" We learned, that day, why Grandma's house is so great. It is where the roots of family go deep and the oneness of the family is felt most deeply. While our condo may be smaller, the size of the dining room will always make it Grandma's house.

21

Can a 'Type A' Ever Be Content?

Just before my father died of a massive heart attack, he sent me a handwritten copy of the prayer, "Slow Me Down, Lord," which is sometimes attributed to Cardinal Richard Cushing. Perhaps, in premonition of his own death, he felt as if his hard-charging son needed the message.

> Slow me down, Lord!
> Ease the pounding of my heart
> by the quieting of my mind.
> Steady my hurried pace
> with the vision of the eternal reach of time.
> Give me, amidst the confusion of the day,
> the calmness of the everlasting hills.
> Break the tensions of my nerves and muscles
> with the soothing music of the singing streams
> that live in my memory.
> Help me to know the magical restoring power of sleep.
> Teach me the art of taking minute vacations…
> of slowing down to look at a flower,
> to chat with a friend,
> to pat a dog,
> to read a few lines from a good book.
> Remind me each day of the fable of the hare and the tortoise,

that I may know that the race is not always to the swift,
that is more to life than measuring its speed.
Let me look upward into the branches of the towering oak
and know that it grew great and strong
because it grew slowly and well.
Slow me down, Lord,
and inspire me to send my roots deep into the soil
of life's enduring values
that I may grow toward the stars of my greater destiny.

I especially love this prayer because it is Dad's legacy to me. From time to time I read it. The beauty and wisdom of its words grip me. But then I put it aside and go charging off again.

If only I could listen and learn.

A Classic "Type A"

Retirement does not guarantee contentment. Even now, I write these words with my emotional engine revving and mental frustration rising.

To know me, you must understand that I am an inveterate doodler. Whenever a pen gets in my hand and paper lies nearby, I doodle. Psychiatrists can quickly analyze my scribbles. Straight lines and arrows betray my personality. I am a self-confessed type A personality — high-energy, hard-charging, goal-oriented, and achievement-driven. When I first learned that I was type A, I wanted to apologize. So, I read the research study that discovered the two types of personalities. As expected, our leaders in business, education, government, and religion tend to be type A.

But with their success comes a price. They are often victims of high blood pressure and heart attacks.

Type B people, on the other hand, are characterized as calm, steady, and satisfied. To me, this seemed to be the better life and more consistent with my Christian faith.

In the next paragraph of the research report I learned that type B people are found most often among undertakers, postal workers, and accountants. That is not who I am and I decided that I was happy to have a type A personality, leading in a stressful job with all of the risks of a heart attack.

Wants that Lure Us

Retirement has its own stress test for a type A personality. What happens when you are no longer leading the parade, charging toward goals, and savoring new achievements? Retirement is like trading a rocket ship for a rocking chair. Can a type A person ever find contentment?

One of the lasting lessons of my high school literature class came from the writings of Henry David Thoreau. When I read *Walden Pond*, I felt as if I were with Thoreau in his hut, listening to the sound of the loons. He seemed to be so content with his simple life. I envied him.

Then, I read his secret for contentment. Thoreau said that wealth is found in reducing the level of your wants to the level of your needs. I took his words and translated them into an equation for contentment:

$$\frac{\text{Wants}}{\text{Needs}} = \text{Contentment}$$

The formula is simple. By dividing our needs into our wants, we determine our level of contentment. When our needs match our wants, contentment comes. The more our wants exceed our needs, the less contented we are. *Ergo*, if we are to be content, we must meet our needs and reduce our wants. Everything in contemporary society works against this formula. Advertising is designed to increase wants beyond our needs, products are manufactured with planned obsolescence so that we will be discontented, and affluence creates an insatiable thirst for sins of luxury. Jesus pointedly addresses these temptations when he says, "Therefore I tell you, do not worry about your life, what you will eat or drink, or about your body, what you will wear. Is not life more important than food, and the body more important than clothes? Look at the birds of the air; they do not sow or reap or store away in barns, and yet your heavenly Father feeds them. Are you not much more valuable than they?" (Matthew 6:25-26).

Do we get the point? Jesus is not talking about lusting for wants, but being anxious about our needs. I suspect that he has the hard-charging, need-anxious, and want-driven type A personality in mind.

Expectations that Drive Us

While we are on the subject of formulas for contentment, William James, the noted psychologist, gives us another. In his study of human personality, he reasoned that emotional health depends upon a match between our expectations and our successes. Translated into a formula for contentment, it would look like this:

$$\frac{\text{Expectations}}{\text{Successes}} = \text{Contentment}$$

The same math applies to this formula that we use for the thinking of Henry David Thoreau. If our successes match our expectations, we are content. If, however, our expectations exceed our successes, we will feel discontent. This is not all bad, because there is a noble discontent that keeps us on the growing edge of personal development. At the same time, we must guard against unrealistic expectations that we can never meet. Neurotics are people who set high expectations for themselves, fail to reach those expectations, and instead of adjusting their goals to coincide with reality, raise them higher and thus assure their failure.

Type A personalities are easy victims of unrealistic expectations. Leaders, in particular, are expected to be insatiable optimists. Because type A personalities often serve in leadership positions, they are particularly vulnerable to the expectations of a glossy view that hides reality. With just a hint of pessimism, the chairman of the Federal Reserve Board can send the stock market into a tailspin.

This is not a plea for lowered expectations. Someone said that if you shoot at a duck, you may miss it, but if you shoot at a skunk, you are bound to hit it. Type A personalities need to be realistic optimists, stretching toward manageable goals with noble discontent, but without the stress of unrealistic expectations.

Circumstances that Plague Us

One more formula comes to mind. The apostle Paul took on the subject of contentment in his letter to the Philippians. He wrote, "I have learned to be content whatever the circumstances. I know what it is to be in need, and I know what it is to have plenty. I have learned the secret of being content in any and every situation, whether well fed or hungry, whether living in plenty or in want. I can do everything through him who gives me strength" (Philippians 4:11-13). I trust that the apostle will forgive me if I reduce his inspired words to a formula for contentment:

$$\frac{\text{Circumstances}}{\text{Trust in God}} = \text{Contentment}$$

Again, the mathematics of the equation looks the same. If our trust equals our circumstances, then we feel content no matter what. But if our circumstances exceed our trust, then circumstances easily overwhelm us.

Unlike the wants and the expectations of our other formulas, we cannot reduce our circumstances. All of us know what Paul means when he says (in a less contemporary version of his message), "I know both how to be abased and I know how to abound" (KJV). As a type A personality, I approach my circumstances with the idea that I change them. But without a trust in God equal to my circumstances, I will soon be overwhelmed.

So, when all is said and done, contentment for a type A personality in retirement is one of our greatest challenges. Our wants continue to lure us, our expectations continue to drive us, and our circumstances continue to plague us. Dare we put the three formulas together and write a workable prescription for contentment?

Reduce our wants,

make our expectations more realistic,

and increase our trust in God.

Type A personalities, take note. There is no other cure for our discontent and no other path to our peace.

22

What If God Says, 'It's None of Your Business'?

I knew that retirement would be a learning experience, but I didn't expect it to include shock treatment.

The physical lessons of aging are tolerable unless a crisis takes health away. Emotional tensions come with the bumps and grinds of changing circumstances, but not usually with a total breakdown. For me, however, the spiritual lesson came when God sent a jolt through my soul. As a person who spent a lifetime trying to obey the will of God, and as a preacher commending his good will to others, I thought that retirement would be a spiritual "walk in the park."

How wrong I was!

Turning Up the Voltage

Do you remember the scene from the television show *E.R.* when the doctor puts paddles on the chest of a patient, asks "Ready?" and then shouts "clear" as the voltage hits the heart and the patient convulses on the table? God has used that kind of shock treatment on my soul during retirement.

It all started when I lost the handle on events that I once controlled. As soon as I retired, my professional ego took a blow when my former colleagues forgot that I existed. At the time of retirement, they promised to keep in touch, seek my counsel, and bring me back for special events. Their promises fell into a deep, dark hole. I felt abandoned.

Another jolt shocked my parental ego as I watched our children raise their families. Sometimes they made financial decisions that curdled my Scotch blood. At other times, discipline of their children went from stern to lax without any apparent consistency. Although I refused to interfere, I could not understand why they didn't follow my example or seek my counsel. I felt neglected.

God had reserved high voltage, however, for my presidential ego. Three or four times since retirement, I have felt as if God put paddles to my chest, turned up the voltage, and yelled "clear!" On each occasion, I overreacted to apparent injustices that stunned my ego. In one instance, I wrote a stinging letter to a landscaping company, urging them to fire their manager for incompetence. Later, I verbally decapitated a fellow director on a board that I chaired for violating privileged communication. Still later, I launched a missile with a nuclear warhead against an embarrassing decision that repudiated action I had taken while still in office. I felt wronged.

Lesser shocks hit my personal ego—overlooked in being invited to the inauguration of a successor, missed in the roll call of special guests at a civic dinner, forgotten in the twenty-fifth anniversary of an organization I founded, ignored in the discussion of historical trends leading to the future, and treated like a delinquent alumnus in an annual fund drive. Admittedly, these are the ruminations of a supersensitive ego, but as I have conversations with other retirees, I find I am not alone in feeling this way.

"Out of sight, out of mind" is the adage that applies to these situations. We all have our tender spots where we feel slighted, even though the oversights may be unintended. On these occasions, all retirees will echo my feelings. We feel hurt.

Counter Shock

Lest this essay degenerate into a "pity party," let me move quickly to the counter shock treatment that God used for my healing. As he does so often, God jolted me with my own words.

If you were to ask me to name one of my favorite stories in Scripture, I would rank close to the top the post-resurrection breakfast encounter between Jesus and Peter. Jesus asks Peter, "Do you love me?" three times, perhaps as a match for the three times that the old fisherman had denied his Lord. After Peter reaffirms his love, Jesus forecasts his future. Comparing youth with old age, Jesus reminds an impulsive and independent man that the time will come when Peter will be dressed by others and led where he does not want to go. Biblical scholars tell us that this was a prediction of death by crucifixion that Peter would suffer in Rome.

But as Jesus concludes his lesson and turns away, Peter looks back at John, the beloved disciple, and calls out to Jesus, "What about *him*?" Intellectually, Peter learns his lesson; but emotionally, Peter is still a control freak. Jesus has to give him a jolt.

"What is that to you?" He asks, flinging the answer back over his shoulder. "Follow me."

Translated into language we can all understand, Jesus tells Peter, "It's none of your business. Follow me."

The End of Egomania

Does God *really* speak like this? You can be sure he does. I know, because that is how he brings me up short when I complain about the blows to the many facets of my tender ego.

Hardly a day goes by that I do not get an e-mail, read an article, see a picture, or hear a rumor that might be conceived as a personal threat. If allowed to fester, these threats could blossom into full-blown paranoia. Retirees, in particular, need to be free from nursing tender egos and worrying about business that now belongs to others.

God's shock treatment saves us from ourselves. If I pursue the issues that damage my ego, nothing but bad blood, deep wounds, and lasting scars will follow. Instead, I must swallow my pride and take God at his word. Nothing—absolutely *nothing*—is worth a break in the relationship of following God. At times, it even gets scary.

In a recent episode after God told me to mind my own business, I bit bullets and showed grace and had the eerie sense that God was honoring my obedience. With shaky pen, I wrote the prediction of a different outcome in the pages of my daybook. A few days later, the prediction came true. While I am not a bleary-eyed mystic or a teary-eyed sentimentalist, I cannot help but believe that God takes control when we give it up.

Bit by bit, I am learning to respond to daily issues as well as ego-bruising problems by anticipating God's response, "What's that to you? Follow me."

Sound easy? It isn't. Because I am slow learner, especially in spiritual things, I know that I will hear God speak again sometime soon when my ego gets entangled in someone else's business.

23

Can a Leopard
Change its Spots?

Jeremiah, the weeping prophet, nearly spits through his teeth when he asks the children of Israel the rhetorical question, "Can an Ethiopian change his skin or the leopard its spots?" (Jeremiah 13:23). The answer, of course, is no.

At best, Jeremiah's answer is cruel humor. To compare Israel's penchant for sinning to the imprint of human nature in the Ethiopian's skin or the leopard's spots is like punching a hole in the life vest of a drowning person. All hope is gone.

The Persistence of Sin

Behind Jeremiah's skeptical query lies an age-old question: Can the persistence of our sins take us past the point of redemption?

Jeremiah is a pessimist. He feels as if the sins of Israel have become so ingrained in the national character that it equals being born that way. This is the Old Testament perspective. A sinner can no more change his ways than an Ethiopian can change his skin or a leopard change its spots. If any passage of Scripture calls out the meaning of grace as unmerited favor, this is the one.

Can we really turn around and go the other way?

As we look at the question in the context of retirement and aging, I want to take a radical position on the question. To begin, I am quick to acknowledge our total depravity as the heirs of Adam and Eve's sin. I am equally quick to believe that the grace of God through the death of Jesus Christ makes our redemption possible. In between the two is where our problem begins. I also believe that human beings have a freedom of will that can frustrate God's desire that everyone believe in him and be saved.

The Way We Walk

At the risk of alienating theological purists, let me bring an experiential perspective into the debate. First, as a psychologist, I accept the viewpoint that our personality is well developed by the age of eleven. Being "born again" makes us a new creature in Christ because our sins are forgiven, but the main characteristics of our personality do not change. A fiery person is still fiery, and a passive person is still passive.

William James's classic work, *The Varieties of Religious Experience*, differentiates between "healthy" and "sick" souls in their conversion.[19] Healthy souls tend to enter the faith without undue trauma. This helps explain why some people profess to be Christians, but cannot remember when they first believed. At the other extreme are sick souls whose sins or personal disposition require a dramatic turnaround in their redemption. Saul's conversion on the Damascus Road, for instance, matches his zeal, hostility, and violence in persecuting Christians. While James's categories may be too neat for the full range of religious experience, they do help us understand how God works within the human personality.

Second, as a hospital chaplain, I learned that traumatic illness does not radically change the character of the person who goes through the experience. Although there may be a temporary reaction called a "deathbed conversion," the patient who survives almost always reverts to his or her long-term character. The same pattern attaches to tragedies that come into our lives. John Claypool, in his book *Tracks of a Fellow Struggler*, tells the story of losing a child to a fatal disease.[20] Often we think that such tragedy brings a husband and wife together. In John's case, however, the struggle exposed the cracks in his marriage and eventually led to divorce. More often than not, personal tragedy speeds us and our relationships in the direction we are already going.

Third, as a retiree entering the ranks of senior citizens, I am witness to the fact that aging does not change our personality or our character. As we grow older, we persist in walking on the same path and in the same direction that we have followed over a lifetime. In fact, the older we get, the more we persist in walking the same path. Psychologists call this "perseveration" in its extreme form.

I recall working with patients in a mental hospital during my clinical training. One woman, a former secretary, spent every waking moment typing on an imaginary keyboard and regularly raising her right hand and snapping her fingers as the signal for the bell at the end of the line. As we age with the blessing of a sound mind, we still tend to persist in patterns of behavior that make us comfortable. Established routines become more important, and established responses become more predictable. Aging proves the point that we are creatures of habit.

Do not get me wrong. I am a firm believer that God can work his miracles in anyone of any age; but without a miracle, personality and character become more and more difficult to change as time goes by.

Another experience comes to mind. When a beloved mother was diagnosed with fast-moving and inoperable cancer, she and her children had different reactions to the news. Following the pattern of a lifetime, she got ready for eternity by setting everything in order, down to the last details of her final arrangements. While all of the children felt crushed by the loss of their mother, they, too, followed the path on which they were already going. Those who had their hope in Christ showed a spurt of spiritual maturity that not only helped them through the crisis, but gave them the opportunity to turn the moment into ministry. Other children who professed no faith went in the opposite direction. They sunk into despair, ran away from their feelings, and blocked out reality. In the end, the differences were highlighted by new spiritual stature for the believers and reinforcement of an old secular spirit for the unbelievers.

The Race to the End

We are persons of free will who make decisions that set a course in life. Jesus minces no words when he says that we will choose the narrow way that leads to eternal life or the broad way that leads to eternal death. Do we have the option of a third way? No. But we can make changes in how we respond.

Grace is full of surprises and we must never fall into the fatal trap of psychological, social, or spiritual determinism.

In retirement, we gather speed in the direction that we are already going. I doubt that we can make a radical change by ourselves. At the very least, we would need intervention as violent as shock treatment to make a turnaround.

Retirement, early or late, is a dress rehearsal for the way we will handle dying and death. Rather than being a U-turn in the path we take, it will be an extension of the direction we have taken throughout our life. The apostle Paul likens life's journey to a track meet in which we are the runners. The race is defined by its stages of preparing, starting, pacing, sprinting, and finishing. From that perspective, Paul's valediction takes on new meaning when he writes, "I have fought the good fight, I have finished the race, I have kept the faith. Now there is in store for me the crown of righteousness" (2 Timothy 4:7-8).

Max DePree adds meaning to the analogy when he says that no one prepares for the one-hundred-yard dash by doing ninety-yard sprints. Rather, the runner practices one-hundred-and-five-yard sprints in order to assure a strong finish.

Think of retirement, then, as sprinting *through* the finish line. It is never too late for the miracle of grace. Repentance and forgiveness—at any age—can set us on course for a crown of righteousness.

24

What Is Red or Blue and Gray all Over?

Is America split between the "red" and the "blue"? According to pundits who followed the election of George W. Bush to a second term in 2004, the nation is almost evenly divided between red conservatives on the right and blue liberals on the left. What is the color of your politics?

If you are red, you are a conservative Republican, usually a fundamentalist Christian, and often an evangelical Christian who supports a right wing agenda of "traditional values." This means that you are pro-life, pro-family, pro-tax cuts, pro-prayer in public schools, pro-Ten Commandments in public places, pro-business, pro-defense, and pro-Israel. James Dobson or the late Jerry Falwell might be your spiritual leader, but Jeff Foxworthy will make you laugh.

With the self-confessed title of a "redneck," Foxworthy pokes fun at hillbillies, trailer courts, six-packs, cars up on blocks, tobacco cuds, and CB radios. Foxworthy's book *You Might Be a Redneck If This Is the Biggest Book You've Ever Read* speaks for itself.

Color Me Red

The small village of Wilmore, Kentucky, lies just south of the sophisticated university town of Lexington, and a stone's throw west from the poverty of the Appalachians. Every day, when Jan and I were living in Wilmore for our career at Asbury Theological Seminary, we saw the clash of cultures.

One morning after a nighttime gusher of rain (for which Kentucky is known), I left the president's office at Asbury Theological Seminary and headed across Lexington Avenue in Wilmore, Kentucky, to speak in the chapel at Asbury College. Fix this image in your mind: I am dressed in the dark blue suit of a preacher with a white shirt, stiff collar, Robert Talbot tie, and tasseled, black loafers. Under my arm I carry my leatherbound Bible and a manila folder holding my speech. For a preacher, I am picture-perfect.

As I cross the street between campuses, I have to step around a huge puddle caused by a clogged storm sewer. No sooner do I reach the other side than a pickup truck hits the puddle, full force. A spray of water explodes from his wheels and swamps me as if it were a small tsunami. Through the water dripping from my eyes, I remember taking one look at the culprit, and the sight is forever imprinted in my brain. I see a grizzled driver with a CAT hat on his head, a gun rack in his rear window, a huge German shepherd in the bed of the truck, and a "Made in America" sticker on his bumper. He looked back with a toothless grin that sent the signal, "the South will rise again." Perhaps in revenge, he thoroughly soaked the left side of my blue-suited preacher's image.

Forgive me for contributing to the stereotype of a redneck! The trademarks of a redneck can be found in any state. The truth is that I love Kentucky, its people, and the strength of its tradition. I will always have a streak of red in me.

The Bluest of the Blue

Retirement changed the color of our political worlds. From the reddest of red in Kentucky, we moved to the bluest of the blue in Seattle, Washington. Name any of the political or morals issues identified by the color red, and a majority of Seattleites will line up at the opposite end of the spectrum.

When we moved back to Seattle, we arrived just in time for some violent protests against the World Trade Organization, life-risking tactics of the Greenpeace society against oil tankers, militant marches for gay rights, the appointment of an active homosexual as dean of St. Mark's Cathedral, the opening of the Music Experience at the Seattle Center (extolling whatever virtues can be found in the drugged mind of Kurt Cobain), the glorification of Seattle grunge, and the election of two female senators proud to display blue.

What a contrast from Kentucky!

Color Me Blue

Don't get me wrong. I also have a solid streak of blue in me. My spiritual forefathers are John Wesley, Francis Asbury, and Benjamin T. Roberts. Each of them preached and practiced the truth that personal holiness is inseparable form social holiness.

Wesley, in eighteenth-century England, led the revival that reformed a nation. Asbury, in nineteenth-century America, championed the cause of the black church. Roberts, founder of the Free Methodist Church in the Civil War period, stood strong for abolition, women's rights, fair labor practices, and the priority of ministry to the poor. To be true to my heritage, I must take on the hues of blue for issues of justice as well as mercy. Whether it is giving priority to the poor, protecting the powerless, providing healthcare for the helpless, preserving the environment or paying down the deficit, my blue streak shows.

The Gray Generation

What have all these political meanderings to do with the subject of retirement? Put in the simplest terms, *the division between red and blue is artificial.*

While there is drama in the extremes, reality gives us a different picture. There are unlimited variations in the Reds and equal differences in the Blues. Surveys show Reds can have streaks of blue, and blues can have spots of red. Evangelical Christians often do not fit well into pigeonholes. A believer who is pro-choice may also be opposed to the death penalty, while an advocate of the family may be a champion of the poor. In politics, a broad broom does not always sweep clean. Retirees come in all shades of political red and blue.

More important than this, *neither red nor blue is a permanent color.* Sooner or later, the red and the blue will turn to gray. Boomers or busters, Generation Xer or millennial, we can't escape the inevitable march of time. The cohort of persons over the age of sixty-five will continue to grow as the bulges of aging generations swell the ranks and people live longer. One of the pivotal questions to ask for the future is, "How will gray power be used to influence the direction and character of the nation?"

As red and blue turn to gray, will this newfound power be used to focus upon selfish ends such as healthcare, Social Security, pension plans, and inheritance taxes? Or will we gain the wisdom of age and experience to address other large and long-term issues such as our legacy to the future? If we are not careful, young radicals become old reactionaries. Oh, to be sure, hardliners with red or blue preferences may take pride in holding a rigid position, but they contribute nothing to public discourse in a lively democracy.

A Telescopic View

What should we expect of the gray generation? First, and foremost, we should expect our elders to bring a *telescopic view* to controversial moral and social issues.

Short-sightedness is the bane of our political existence. When pursuing politics as the "art of the possible," there is always the temptation to sacrifice the long-term good for short-term gains. Social Security reform is a case in point. For those of us who are beneficiaries of Social Security, the threat of bankruptcy in 2040 is beyond our lifetime. It is easy to adopt a short-term perspective, enjoy the benefits, and let future generations handle future problems. The wisdom of age, however, should give us a sense of responsibility for our children and grandchildren.

I think of the analogy of the olive tree. Because it grows slowly from a miniscule seed, the generation that plants the tree will never eat from its fruit. Retirees need to take this long-term view in every decision we make. If our goals are merely short-term and our aims are exclusively selfish, we are not worthy to be called "senior" citizens.

A Kaleidoscopic View

Next, as members of the gray generation, we need to bring to the table of public discourse a *kaleidoscopic view*. Although seeing the "big picture" has become a cliché in leadership language, it is still a lens through which we can see that the whole is greater than the sum of the parts.

As in a child's kaleidoscope, a turn of the lens scatters all the pieces, but it also reconfigures the pieces into an integrated design. While in career, our attention remains fixed on the details; in retirement, we have the time to reflect upon the larger scene and make some sense of its meaning. To achieve this perspective, we need a focus from which to see the whole. Without a focus, there is no integration and there is no wholeness.

The abortion question comes to mind. From the foes of abortion comes an appeal to the "sanctity of life." Well said. The "sanctity of life" gives us a focused lens through which we can view the many controversies scattered on the landscape of the abortion issue. Yet a problem arises when we limit the "sanctity of life" to the beginning of human existence. If this happens, we become guilty of saying that life begins at conception and ends at birth. Senior citizens should be the first to call this viewpoint into question.

Regardless of whether we agree with the Roman Catholic position on abortion, we can commend Cardinal Bernardin of Chicago for seeing the sanctity of life as a "seamless garment" which begins at conception and ends at death. It is not uncommon for civilizations to lose respect for the elderly and shuttle them aside as worthless. As a case in point, elderly abuse is almost as common in our society as child abuse. Every senior citizen has a stake in seeing the sanctity of life as a seamless garment. So, whatever the issue—whether abortion or abuse, stem cell research or cloning, adoption or poverty, capital punishment or euthanasia—we need to be unwaveringly consistent, keeping our focus on the whole and not on individual issues.

A Gyroscopic View

A mature viewpoint is balanced as well as far-sighted and whole. The wisdom of age and experience should therefore give us a *gyroscopic view* of contending issues that can throw a society out of balance.

The competitive forces of gravity and motion stabilize a spinning gyroscope. The greater the stress, the faster it spins; the faster it spins, the more stable it is. Red conservatives and blue liberals are like the opposing forces of a gyroscope in which an immovable object meets an irresistible force. This is especially true in the social arena where conservative Christians are known for "mercy" and liberal Christians consider themselves champions of "justice."

When it comes to programs of mercy for human suffering across the world, conservative Christians are the undisputed leaders. World Vision, World Relief, and World Concern are examples of the thousands of "faith-based" ministries of compassion for the poor and needy of the world. Suffering individuals tug at the hearts of conservative Christians. "One Soul at a Time," the watchword for missions and evangelism in my denomination, tells the story. The underlying assumption is that redemption is an individual matter.

With equal strength of conviction, liberal Christians find hope for suffering individuals in changes within the systems that cause the pain. For these Christians, a change in the structure and systems of society—not just in programs of evangelism and relief—is the remedy to suffering. Justice rings loudly in their agenda. Whether it is priorities in the federal budget, protection of the poor in human welfare, issues of human rights in the courts, or contests for the freedom of speech in the media, justice must be done. Standing in sharp contrast to conservative Christians, liberal Christians first see human redemption in radical changes in social systems—beginning with government—rather than in individual salvation.

Neither side is wholly right. Christ's message changes individual persons *and* challenges social systems. Our Christian witness is both personal *and* social. Who can bring this balance to our twenty-first-century ministry? Just as the politics of the nation is split between the red and the blue, evangelical Christians are being split between activists who make right-wing politics a litmus test for the faith, and those who condemn a lack of passion for the poor, a lack of discipline for the sins of self-indulgence, and a lack of difference-making in the statistics of secular attitudes and actions.

The gray generation has nothing to lose in calling for a balance between the red and blue. No one disputes that both sin and salvation are personal and social. Politics push people to the extremes and prejudice puts them into pigeonholes. Those who call for balance are often labeled as rabble-rousers, traitors, and heretics. But someone needs to take the risk, step into the gap, and set the gyroscope spinning. If not the seniors of the gray generation, then who?

As it stands now, the voice of wisdom has been stilled by the postmodern attitude that puts seniors on the shelf. Somehow, we need to find our voice and speak our mind.

25

Is 'Senior Spirituality' Something Special?

Young Americans amaze us. Just when we think that they have succumbed to the sirens of secularism, Associated Press surveys show that four of five college freshmen have an interest in spirituality. Forty-four percent of eighteen- to twenty-five-year-olds also call themselves "religious" and an additional 35 percent say that they are "spiritual, but not religious."[21]

What in the world is going on?

The Thirst for Secular Spirituality

In our generation, spirituality is both vogue and vague. The subject has become so popular that bookstores now have a special section reserved for books on spirituality quite set apart from works on religion.

A quick look at the sections in Barnes and Noble will tell you that spirituality is a subject of its own, with a direct connection to the New Age movement (which, incidentally, gets more shelf space than Christianity). Or try the CD section, in which you will find a full rack of discs that promise to help you with everything from "spiritual chill-out" to "spiritual healing."

If you go online to Amazon.com, you will find thousands of volumes dedicated to the subject of "spirituality." While many of the books are written from a Christian perspective, the subject has been stretched far beyond its traditional meaning. There is spirituality for people of every age—children, teens, people in mid-life, and the elderly. No ethnic setting is left out—African, Celtic, Jewish, Islamic, Asian, or Native American searchers can find specialties on spirituality for women, nomads, gays, environmentalists, and street kids.

Marketers will be pleased to know that spirituality can be sold; wine-drinkers will enjoy the connection with "spirits"; busy people will discover shortcuts to the goal; astrologers will see spirituality's meaning in the stars; health nuts will reap spirituality's benefits; and dummies will learn the basics without sweat.

Like the coin of the realm during an inflationary spiral, spirituality has been devalued in the marketplace. Yet the popularity of the subject reveals the strong spiritual thirst of our generation.

Christian Spirituality Comes of Age

Over the years, I have watched the meaning of Christian spirituality go through subtle but significant change. Until thirty or forty years ago, the subject belonged to ancients in the desert or monks in the monastery. Spirituality meant self-denial of the flesh as the path to godliness. Thomas á Kempis's book *The Imitation of Christ* is a textbook for monastic spirituality.

The term took a turn in the 1960s when evangelical Christianity leaned toward the charismatic movement. Spirituality came to mean cultivating the special gifts of the Spirit as the means of growing in grace. Then, in the 1980s, seminaries began to realize that future ministers needed more than an *understanding* of the faith; they needed to *experience* the faith in depth. The seminary where I served as president led the way by opening the first Department of Prayer and Spiritual Life to exist in Protestant theological education.

"Spiritual Formation" is the term used to describe this new emphasis. Drawing from Roman Catholic and Orthodox traditions, the term implies spiritual growth based upon the building blocks of devotion—including prayer, Bible study, fasting, and solitude.

Knowledge of the need for this spread to the laity, and Richard Foster responded with a book that became a classic, *The Celebration of Discipline.* Spirituality thus shifted from "formation" to "discipline."

Although the difference between the terms may be subtle, the notion of spiritual formation seems less threatening than spiritual discipline. When we think about discipline, our mind might immediately conjure up the image of a diet combined with exercise. And just as people buy diet and exercise books by the millions at the same time that we are getting fatter and fatter, Christians buy millions of books on spiritual discipline but live more and more like secularists.

Lately, the wind has shifted again. Perhaps in reaction against the potentially negative connotation of "discipline," we are seeing the term "spiritual transformation" taking hold. Spirituality, even within Christian ranks, has taken on a life of its own. It has become a specialty with a customized fit for theological, cultural, and generational differences.

Is "senior spirituality" one of those specialties?

Senior Spirituality

Age and spirituality are supposed to grow together. As we age, we are expected to grow closer to God, see his vision, obey his commands, understand his ways, show his compassion, practice his patience, and speak his wisdom. Retirement, presumably, gives us the time to become models of spirituality. We should be able to capitalize on years of growth, formation, discipline, and transformation.

If only this were true!

From my experience in retirement, *spirituality* defined in modern terms is still an elusive dream. In the sixty-four years since my conversion, my idea of spirituality has grown far more practical, more religious, more creedal, and decidedly more earthbound than the widespread contemporary quest. If I were to write a book on spirituality for seniors, it would be tied to the Word of God, related to a community of faith, responsive to an historic Christian creed, worked out in the most mundane of human affairs, and especially tied to a system of accountability.

Upholding this model may well be the greatest contribution that senior citizens can make in the current quest for spirituality. Away with the ambiguity, down with the pretty words, up with the radical vow. Stop at the place where the rubber meets the road, and answer to those you can trust.

God truly is in the everyday details. I love the image of Brother Lawrence finding spirituality among dirty pots and pans, or Teresa of Avila seeing God while chomping on a chicken leg. We, who are senior citizens in the Christian faith, need to dispel the notions that spirituality is as ambiguous as the wash of a watercolor painting, as private as solitary faith, as pluralistic as many world religions, and as idealistic as a figment of the imagination.

For what it is worth, I offer the following definition of spirituality. Admittedly, it may not pass the test of philosophical, psychological, or sociological definitions, but I am willing to let it be judged by the standard of Christ's teachings. *Spirituality is the result of radical obedience to Jesus Christ and his teachings.*

John Stott confesses that his favorite verses in Scripture are found in John 14, where Jesus says, "If you love me, you will obey what I command" (John 14:15). Jesus is not talking about *qualified* obedience. He shows us the way in his *total* obedience to the words and ways of the Father. So away with our self-styled definitions of spirituality! Simple obedience to the Word of God in Christ is uncluttered and uncontaminated spirituality.

Think of it this way: spirituality is more practical than mystical, more relational than independent, and more external than internal. Above all, it is not something we can gain by self-denial, self-formation, or self-discipline. At best, these approaches will leave us as frustrated as Benjamin Franklin when he tried to hone his life to perfect with a rigorous discipline of self-improvement. Eventually, he gave up, likening himself to a man who wanted the entire head of his ax to be as bright as the edge, but who later gave up on the sharpening process, saying, "I think I like a speckled ax best."

Seniors have an advantage. We have seen the quest for spirituality go through stage after stage over a long span of years. Far more humble now, we know that spirituality is a gift of grace, not a work of grit. So as a word to future generations, we offer the truth of Scripture that transcends every technique:

> Now the Lord is the Spirit, and where the Spirit of the Lord is, there is freedom. And we, who with unveiled faces all reflect the Lord's glory, are being transformed into his likeness with ever-increasing glory, which comes from the Lord, who is the Spirit. (2 Corinthians 3:17-18)

No scriptural passage is more clear. Christian spirituality is being free in the Spirit, reflecting God's glory, and being transformed into the likeness of God's Son. None of this is our doing. It comes from the Lord, who is the Spirit.

Whether seniors or juniors, this is our quest.

PART VI

Lean Forward

26

Who Says
You Can't Take It with You?

Good comedy contains a germ of truth. Johnny Carson, on his *Tonight Show*, once quipped, "I have never seen a hearse on the Los Angeles freeway towing a U-Haul trailer." In his inimitable way, Carson confirmed the adage, "You can't take it with you."

An up-to-date variation on the same theme is a T-shirt imprinted with the words, "He Who Dies with the Most Toys....Still Dies." As proof of our age of affluence, earthly possessions—houses, land, furnishings, and jewels—are now called "big boy toys" or "big girl toys," along with stereos, cell phones, digital cameras, Game Boys, and iPods.

Instead of keeping up with the Joneses, we are trying to keep with the Gateses.

Add to our toys the clutter of "stuff" housed in self-storage units across the country. A seventeen-*billion*-dollar industry has resulted from the junk we have collected but cannot use. But the adage still holds: You can't take it with you.

Or can you?

Beyond Possessions and Toys

Believe it or not, there is an exception. Retirees of our generation face a new reality—beyond possessions and toys—about life after death.

We are the generation that has accumulated wealth far beyond all expectation.

At one time, only the very wealthy worried about their estates after death. Today, wealth has spread to millions of hard-working and frugal people who have become investors in the market and winners of economic growth. Consequently, the transfer of wealth from our generation to our children will be the greatest in human history thus far. Estimates of that transfer run as high as thirty-three *trillion* dollars, depending upon fluctuations in the marketplace.[22] And by 2052, when the boomers pass on their wealth, the amount is projected at 41 trillion dollars.[23] Frightening questions follow:

- Who will inherit the wealth?
- Will our heirs be wise or wasteful with wealth they have not earned?
- What is our responsibility to assure that our wealth perpetuates our moral and spiritual values?

For some reason, retirees are reluctant to ask or answer these big questions. Perhaps we do not want to face our own mortality. Or is it simply too much bother to get into the details of estate planning? Whatever the case, we sin against the future if we do not accept responsibility for the transfer of our wealth.

One sin is *to die "intestate,"* meaning to die without taking the time to plan our estate and write our will. Irony reigns when a person who complains about big government dies intestate and leaves most of the money to fund that government. A will is a declaration of intent that perpetuates our convictions and our values to the next generation.

Another sin is *to die self-serving.* How often have you heard young, self-indulgent executives say that they plan to make a major gift to charity *in the future*? It will never be. Unless we *live* as givers, we will never *die* as givers.

Still another sin is *to spoil our children*. I can still hear my father saying, "From shirtsleeves to shirtsleeves in three generations." It is still true. One generation earns the wealth, the second generation spends it, and the third generation has to start all over again. Today's retirees have the responsibility to teach their children the discipline of finance in order to avoid the squandering of their money.

One wealthy couple in our neighborhood has four children, lives in a million-dollar home, and travels worldwide without blinking an eye. I saw the preteen daughter one day as she was walking a dog I had never before seen. When I asked her if she got a new dog, she answered, "No, it isn't my dog. I walk her every day. This is my job." In that answer, I saw the home life of the family unfold. Every child has a job that brings in cash or a chore that determines allowance. And as rich as the family is, the children are courteous, unspoiled, and happy.

Our Debt to the Future

I never thought I would have to worry about planning our estate. At first, I only wanted to assure retirement income and long-term health care. This initial planning paid off when we were blessed to catch the high tide of pension funds, property values, and the stock market during the 1990s. So in retirement, lifetime security advances to long-term planning.

My first priority is *to assure adequate income to meet expenses for a standard of living that will encompass both our expected life spans.* Resource planning also includes the provision for long-term care, in the event that is needed.

Close behind this first priority is my desire *to protect my wife from the dangers of being bilked if I die first.* A large majority of the funds in the 41 trillion-dollar transfer of wealth will be in the hands of women, most of whom will be widows because women generally live longer than men. A widow may be left at loss on how to proceed, and thus, vulnerable to scams or amateur advice. She may need the protection of trusted advisors who can help her make wise decisions on financial planning. This is what I call the "tipping point" for Christian stewardship in the future. If there is one financial priority for Christian stewardship for tomorrow, it is to assure that widows can direct their funds to economical and effective ministries, ones without the heavy cost of a rake-off for management.

Right after this comes the desire *to provide for the needs of our children.* Because we know that nothing splits a family like money, we are cautious in providing for their welfare. Frankly, we would rather help them during the start of their families and by giving gifts in the time of need than to leave them an undesignated bundle later on. Because their needs change from time to time, we will continue to monitor the provisions of the will and remain flexible for change.

In recent days I have been thinking again about the principle of perpetuating our spiritual commitment through estate planning. Throughout our lives, Jan and I paid a tithe on our gross income. When our children took their first jobs, we encouraged them to follow our example. How, then, do we perpetuate that principle in the gifts that we will bestow from our estates?

Although I have not yet checked out all of the legal and financial implications of my decision, I want to write into our will the stipulation that any gifts to future generations be tithed by the beneficiaries to the ministries we supported during our lifetime. Is this too controlling? I think not. Isn't it a way to teach biblical stewardship even after our death? I want to leave the legacy of tithing to the next generation.

Our Eternal Investment

What about an eternal investment? So far, I have been talking about the resources we will leave behind. Is it possible that we can make lifetime decisions that have eternal consequences?

We usually think of these decisions in the light of judgment. I still cringe when I think back to the children's Sunday school class where the teacher told the story of the rich man who said, "'I will tear down my barns and build bigger...and I'll say to myself, "You have plenty of good things laid up for many years. Take life easy; eat, drink and be merry."' "But God said to him, 'You fool! This very night your life will be demanded from you. Then who will get what you have prepared for yourself?'" The teacher stopped there, but should have told the rest of the story. Jesus concluded with the moral, "This is how it will be with anyone who stores up things for himself but is not rich toward God" (Luke 12:18-21).

How, then, can we be rich toward God? If selfish investments bring God's judgment, why not believe that selfless investments bring God's wealth? John Wesley, the founder of Methodism, is a model for me. He is well-known for admonishing his people, "Make all you can, save all you can, give all you can." Wesley walked his talk. At the height of his ministry in eighteenth-century England, he had earnings that would have made him one of the richest men in the country. Instead of accumulating his wealth, however, he gave away everything except the amount of money required to meet his basic needs — and that salary did not vary over the years of his ministry.

John Wesley anticipated the advice that Henry David Thoreau gave his readers a century later when he said that we make ourselves rich by making our wants few. This is the formula for the riches of God. Meeting our needs, reducing our wants, and giving all we can will bring wealth beyond measure.

Give While You Can

Although I believe in estate planning to fulfill our wishes after death, I find more joy in giving from the estate when we can. Hugh White, chairman of the board for my first college presidency, said he gained satisfaction and had fun seeing his gifts at work. During their lifetimes, he and his wife, Edna, gave and gave and gave as major donors to their local church, world missions, and Spring Arbor College.

Taking a cue from him, my wife and I try to put together gift packages for people and programs. This becomes our living endowment. I can honestly say that the greatest joy in giving is to receive a note of thanks from a student helped by a scholarship, or to see the radiant face of an Indian child whom we sponsor.

Jesus did not limit his stories about eternal investments to rich men who built bigger barns, people who turned away from the poor, or those who scoffed at roadside beggars. He also said that a cup of cold water given in his name would not be forgotten. Our unconscious compassion for the poor, the naked, and the imprisoned, Jesus said, would be recognized upon our entry into the kingdom of God.

Retirement is the time to claim these promises. You *can* take it with you.

27

What's So Bad about Green Bananas?

When a stockbroker tried to get an eighty-five-year-old woman to make a long-term investment, she retorted, "Sonny, I'm so old...I don't even buy green bananas."

Her snippy response characterizes the attitude of an age when human existence gets squeezed into the present moment of time.

People of ancient civilizations never thought this way.

Plan for the Generations

When my son and I visited the Garden of Gethsemane on the Mount of Olives, our guide told us that some of the gnarled olive trees were there when Jesus prayed for the final time before his arrest, trial, and crucifixion. The guide also told us that an Israeli farmer never expects to eat the fruit of the trees he plants. He works so that his children, grandchildren, and future generations will enjoy the olives.

Do we only buy ripe bananas or do we plant olive trees? This is one of our choices when we retire. Will we shorten or lengthen our plan for the future as we grow older?

Charlie Spicer, founding chair for Overseas Council International, taught me the answer. When I asked what he was doing for his sixty-fifth birthday, he perked up and said, "I'm making thirty-year year plans!" Since that time, Charlie has been diagnosed with cancer throughout his body, including vital organs. According to his doctor, his life span was limited to six months. Yet between heavy, multiple doses of chemotherapy, he and his wife continued their tireless travel around the world on behalf of Overseas Council, visiting the theological seminaries and raising scholarship monies. Outliving the doctor's prognosis by an extra year, he flew to meet a donor for a major gift just two weeks before his death. In his last hours he asked his son-in-law to remind the donor of his promise. Who can doubt a direct connection between his thirty-year plans and the lengthening of his life?

I am well aware of research that finds no connection between a delay in death from cancer and the anticipation of major holidays, such as a birthday, Thanksgiving, and Christmas. And I know that it is not scientifically sound to argue from individual cases. But until the evidence in refutable, I will always contend that there exists a direct connection between the length of our plans and the length of our life.

Someone has said that our fiftieth birthday is critical because we realize that most of our life is behind us. The psalmist writes, "The length of our days is seventy years—or eighty, if we have the strength" (Psalm 90:10). At each of these milestones, we have to decide whether our life is opening up or closing down.

Reality pushes us to face the fact that we die a bit at a time as we age. One by one, our physical, mental, and emotional agilities decline. Sometimes this happens sooner rather than later.

The best athletes in the world retire in their thirties, when they lose a half step of speed on the court or a couple miles an hour on a fast ball. In their autobiographies, they often liken their loss to a form of death. Like death, one world passes away and another one comes into view. Also, like death, most athletes are not prepared for the change. Suddenly their identity is no longer tied to their sports image and their role is no longer defined by their performance on the field. Retirement from stardom in athletics, entertainment, or prestige positions has much in common with Psychiatrist Elisabeth Kübler-Ross's theory of death and dying: Denial, anger, negotiation, and acceptance are all part of the process.[24]

As we age, the losses are larger and more frequent. No wonder we feel tempted to take the view that life is closing down and conclude with the pessimist, "As for man, his days are like grass, he flourishes like a flower of the field; the wind blows over it and it is gone, and its place remembers it no more" (Psalm 103:15-16).

At the same time, we must also admit that our future planning is based upon the assumption that we will have the physical, mental, and emotional agilities to realize our dream. This is the crux of the problem. As we age and our agilities decline, we assume that long-range planning also declines.

Nothing is further from the truth.

I will buy green bananas as long as I live. In fact, I will champion this principle: *The older we grow, the longer we plan.* Because I am a minister, my readers will expect me to write a homily about the extension of long-range planning into eternity. Sorry, dear friends, that comes later! Right now, as I hit the mid-range between the biblical promise of seventy and eighty, I am making very mundane and unspiritual plans:

- I will start playing doubles in tennis when I reach my eighties.
- I will have my crooked front teeth veneered with porcelain and live long enough to amortize the cost.
- I will travel with our son to India for the dedication of the children's hostels that we helped fund.
- I will continue to write a book a year from the unwritten stories still in my head.

Do these plans sound silly or selfish? Perhaps and perhaps not. They deserve a second look before judgment is pronounced.

Tennis for Two?

I have played tennis all of my life. High on the shelf in my study are four silver trophies from my competitive days. We are a tennis family with one son a teaching pro, one granddaughter a state champion, and one grandson currently ranked as a sixteen-year-old player in his home state.

When we bought our retirement home in Seattle, a tennis court beckoned a mere fifty steps from our front door. To tell the truth, the sight of the tennis court marked "For Residents Only" cinched the decision to buy the home. Whenever the family gets together, we have rousing matches of competition. So why not keep the dream alive?

My mental tennis is as sharp as ever, even though my feet find it hard to obey. On the tennis court I come alive, and win or lose, I leave refreshed. At this point, I can still play a fair game of singles, but not without long-lasting aches and pains. Sooner or later, realism will set in and I will have to settle for being a partner in a doubles game that cuts the size of the court in half.

My competitive nature, however, sees that as a compromise. So my goal is to keep playing singles through my seventies. Wait! That's not me. If this old body permits, I will celebrate my eightieth birthday by challenging one of our kids to a game of singles.

Toothy Smile?

Okay, I admit that getting my front teeth capped betrays my vanity. Sixty years ago, I chipped my front tooth in a high school football game. The ragged edge shows in every portrait or snapshot. The bottom front teeth are even worse. And because my parents could not afford braces, crooked teeth have never been straightened.

I really didn't think about getting any work done on my teeth until I posed for a publicity shot at the request of a publisher. Very diplomatically, she rejected a shot that had been taken ten years ago, just before the streaks of gray became white and the face had the non-wrinkled look of an airbrush job. When I saw the newer photograph I had taken, I rebelled. My teeth, in particular, had the yellowed look of an inveterate coffee drinker and the chipped and crooked look of a guy who could have posed for the "Before" picture in an orthodontist's ad. So, saving the nickels from consulting fees and royalty payments, I put together an "extreme makeover" fund for recapping my front teeth.

It worked.

The process was painless, but time-consuming and costly. Now my goal is to show my pearly porcelains in our sixtieth wedding anniversary photo. When the photographer says "smile," I will give it my best.

India at Last?

A mission to India has been a deferred, long-range goal for fifty years. When I was a senior in seminary, a missionary from India came to our chapel and asked for volunteers who would visit that distant land.

Because I was on a fast track toward my Ph.D., I rebelled against the thought of giving up my academic future. After a struggle of wills, I decided that I would let go of my plans in favor of God's good will. I prayed, "Lord, I will go to India if that is your will, even if I never get the Ph.D." That decision made, I was set free. A new path opened to the Ph.D. and I began a career in Christian higher education—but always under the mandate of readiness to go to India if God should call.

In 1980, after I missed the appointment as secretary of education in the Reagan cabinet, I was asked if there were any other position in which I might be interested. Foolishly, but faithfully, I answered, "Yes—Ambassador to India." The appointment never came, but I have said time and time again, "The call to India has never been canceled. If God should issue the order, I would be on the first plane out."

After Jan and I retired, the challenge returned in the call to rebuild six hostels for 600 Indian children. The children were being sent by their parents to the hostels primarily for education, but also for Christian training. The story gripped our heart and we proposed the project for the Christian fellowship we had become a part of in our suburban neighborhood. The members responded by meeting the $37,000 goal for remodeling the hostels, as well as sponsoring more than one hundred of the children.

Then, I received an invitation to be present at the dedication of the hostels upon the completion of the work. Although I was tired of world travel, I could not resist this invitation. And Jan agreed that I could go, only if our younger son, Rob, could accompany me. (Naturally, she has concerns about a husband with a history of heart disease!) A lifetime commitment came back into focus for me, and joyfully I responded, "Yes!" I could still answer the call that I first heard fifty years ago.

The Next Book?

A child who was a prodigy in art was asked, "Which of your paintings is the best?" He answered, "The best is still in my head."

I feel that way about the books I write. To date, twenty-five books have flowed from my pen, with two more contracted for publication. None is a bestseller, but each has served its purpose of expressing my mind and heart with a word of encouragement for my readers. Which of these books is the best? Like the child artist, I answer, "The best is still in my head."

If you were to ask me about the next book I want to write, I will give you at least five or six tentative titles rumbling around in my mind. Because my life's mission is to integrate Christian faith with human learning, each book will be variation on that theme and a direct reflection of my experience.

Executive leadership, of course, is my forte. If I learned nothing worthy of being passed on to the next generation after thirty-three years as a president in higher education, then my years were wasted. In the beginning, I am sure I was absorbed with the details of everyday survival. As the years passed, those details came together to form principles, and then those principles merged into insights with moral and spiritual dimensions. It is these insights that may have some value for today's executive leaders, whether in higher education, religion, business, or government.

The titles are all in my mind—but I will not reveal them. Without the advantage of a magic name such as Philip Yancey or the media audience of Chuck Swindoll, I have to count on the title to get my books off the shelf. That explains why one of my books carries the title *Never Blink in a Hailstorm*. It also explains why I chose the name *Retirement Is Not for Sissies* for the book you are reading. Other creative titles are in the offing; I want them to come as a surprise in the marketplace.

If I continue to write a book a year, it will take me at least five or six years to complete the next phase of my writing. By that time, I expect there will be *another* five or six books in my head.

Can I continue to write into my eighties and beyond? Why not? Grandma Moses, who came into her prime when she was in her eighties, is my model. I will *not* be like the preacher of whom a parishioner said, "Each sermon that you preach is better than the next one." No way! Exercising the principle behind buying green bananas, my best book will always be the one in my head.

From Here to Eternity?

"What about eternity?" you ask. "How does this schedule fit your long-range planning?" I imagine that you expected me to write this chapter with eternity in view. Instead, I have confessed that my primary interest is on future goals anchored to earth.

I do not apologize.

Although I have been a Christian minister for more than fifty years, I still do not have a functional grasp on eternity. To be sure, I know the Scriptures and I know the promises. I accept them by faith and anticipate their fulfillment. Yet my approach to eternity goes through the mundane.

As I anticipate the future and my entrance into eternity, I do not expect some cataclysmic event to bring me into the presence of the King. Instead, I hope to walk one step at a time, never ceasing to make earthly goals, until I reach God's home. At that moment, I pray that the invitation will come to take the final step into eternity, a future without an end.

Green bananas are totally consistent with that hope.

28

Can a Checkout Counter
Be a Bully Pulpit?

Before I retired, groceries simply appeared on the kitchen
counter, disappeared into the refrigerator, and reappeared on
the dining table. After retirement, all of this changed.

I became acquainted with my wife's sophisticated system
of planning meals, taking a daily inventory of the pantry, preparing a list of needs, scheduling a shopping trip, scanning the
aisles for items, checking the labels for trans fat, loading the
basket, standing in line, sliding a debit card through the slot,
asking for paper bags, and chatting with the bagger on the way
to the car.

Today I know the truth: Grocery shopping is a joint venture for retired couples.

The Burberry Scarf

The first time I went through the experience of grocery shopping with my wife, my CEO mentality made me impatient with
the time she took to compare prices and nutrients on breakfast
cereals. Why not choose my morning favorite and let it go at
that?

This was just the beginning. Every purchase had to pass the scrutiny of an eye practiced in the art of comparison-shopping for price and value. Awed by her process, I pushed the cart through the aisles and to the checkout line, thinking I had found my chance to take over!

Hoping to secure a quick exit, I cast a practiced, executive eye at the checkout-line options, and darted to a position in line in front of a woman with a baby. Only a gray-haired lady with an English wool hat and a Burberry scarf around her neck stood ahead of us. She appeared neat and tidy, and I expected efficiency in the final transaction. So, after establishing the boundary for our groceries with a divider stick on the conveyor belt, I did my husbandly duty by unloading the food items, one at a time, and then settled back to await our turn.

All went well until the woman ahead of us pulled out a checkbook to pay her bill. She wrote ever so slowly. After asking the date and writing some more, she turned to the back of the checkbook to record the transaction equally slowly before handing the check to the clerk. I felt a growl of anxiety inside: *Why doesn't she do her homework after she leaves?* When she finally handed over the check, the clerk asked for identification.

Confused, the woman reached into her handbag and extracted a wallet, but could not find her driver's license. While I fumed inside, I looked up to see the woman with the baby leaving the checkout counter next to us and tossing a sweet smile in my direction. Grrrrr! That did it. I was about to make some disparaging remark under my breath, when the woman ahead of us turned and said in a plaintive voice, "I'm so sorry."

While I smiled weakly in response, my wife, Jan, chirped, "That's okay. We're retired."

In an instant, everyone at the checkout counter—customers, clerk, even I—had to laugh.

The woman replied, "So am I."

The clerk said, "I wish I were."

And the person in line behind us added, "You are *so* lucky."

A magical minute followed. Jan described how much fun we had shopping together; the woman revealed that she was a widow; and the clerk let us know that she was divorced. Shame and pride crowded into my soul. My shame was in my impatience; my pride was in my wife. She taught me the meaning of being fully alive in every moment that we live. She had turned a garrulous checkout line into a bully pulpit!

The Henna Solution

After the humility of that lesson, I decided I wanted to learn more about my wife's ministry at a checkout counter. Following her into a drugstore one day, I watched her go through the routine of a woman "born to shop."

When she reached the checkout line, a squatty woman with a timeworn face and a henna hairdo called out, "Come over to my line."

Jan obeyed while pointing to the woman and saying, "This is my friend."

I couldn't believe what I just heard. My wife asked the woman whether she had resolved a conflict with her sister and how the woman's mother was doing. In turn, the woman knew about our trip to Hawaii and our move to a new condo. In a ministry of moments, Jan responded to the woman's report on the unresolved conflict with the sister by saying, "I'll pray for you," and adding "Praise the Lord" when she heard that her mother was doing better.

Me? I was ducking my head. My idea of a public Christian witness did not include "Praise the Lord!" for all to hear.

How wrong I was! No one else seemed to mind what Jan said; in fact, the whole place brightened with smiles as the woman said "thank you," and added, "Your husband makes a good carryout boy."

It was my turn. A spiritually challenged bagger carried our groceries to the car in humble silence while Jan chatted cheerfully about the woman whom she had called "my friend."

The Judgment Seat

How can something so mundane as a checkout counter be a spiritual test? After seeing the affirmative example in the joyful spirit of my wife, I remembered the number of times that we had gone through the checkout line at a grocery store that served primarily an adult community of residents fifty-five years and older.

Sullen customers stood silently in line without acknowledging the shoppers behind or ahead of them. When they arrived at the pay station, they grunted at the cheerless "hello" of the clerk, scowled at the machine registering each item, grumbled at their spouse, and usually found something about which to complain. Never in my life have I seen such regular displays of unhappiness. Something about grocery shopping brought out the worst in these people, and the checkout counter became the judgment seat. All of the catch phrases about "crotchety old codgers" proved true.

No wonder that one bright soul uttering the simple words, "That's okay; we're retired," is a ministry in itself.

As I dug deeper into the meaning of this experience, I think I might have discovered why a checkout counter becomes a seat of judgment. First, *retirement makes us stop and think.*

Despite all our efforts to fill up the time and keep busy, retirement is a time when you *have* to stop and think. Nothing is more dangerous. Whether we are early retirees in our fifties or standard retirees in our sixties, we come to realize that the longest part of our life is behind us. Consequently, we get caught between what Henri Nouwen calls the "ought" and the "if."[25]

Remembering our past, we see what we ought to have done and what we ought not to have done. Sins of omission and commission become hounds that dog our feet. Then, when we look forward, all of the "ifs" of the future arise like ghosts to haunt us. We dare not stop for a moment without confronting our immortality. Regrets for the past and fears for the future wither the spirit and suffocate the joy. Disgruntled souls hate a checkout counter because they cannot avoid coming face-to-face with another human being. Perhaps the newer self-service lines that limit interaction to a faceless machine were invented to save the sanity of such unhappy individuals.

Second, *retirement tests our self-esteem.* Without the artificial bolstering of career for our egos, retirement exposes how we feel about ourselves and how we think that people feel about us. We get what we anticipate. If we have a positive self-image, then we expect other people to respond positively to us. If we carry a negative self-image, we believe that other people do not care about us. Whether in the little snits of disgruntlement or in the extreme depths of depression, we reinforce the negative in all of our relationships.

A key test for our self-esteem is how we handle compliments. If we have high self-esteem, we take compliments with a gracious "thank you." But a low self-esteem prompts us to either reject the compliment or divert it with a lame excuse.

Whether we know it or not, a rejection or diversion of a compliment demeans the person who gave it. Just the opposite is true when we respond with a, "Oh, thank you! That makes my day." Like a touch of grace, the self-worth of both parties is lifted and they look forward to meeting again.

A checkout counter is a perfect place to test our self-esteem by compliments.

Third, *retirement shows our faith*. Only faith can save us from being victims whip-sawed between the *ought* and the *if*. By trusting in Christ, forgiveness cancels the power of ought and hope takes away the dread of if. That is when we discover the meaning of *is*.

In Ephesians and Philippians, the apostle Paul repeatedly emphasizes that we are alive in Christ and living fully in the present, with no regret for the forgiven past or fear of the unknown future. How better to capture the vibrancy of being "in Christ" than by speaking the lilting words, "That's okay; we're retired"? I witnessed faith coming alive when I heard Jan speak those words in the humdrum of a checkout line where everything (in my estimation) was going wrong. Because Jan's life is centered in Christ and she is secure in the presence of God, an epiphany took shape in a checkout line.

The Sound of Singing

At the center of the campus at Spring Arbor University, just west of the city of Jackson, Michigan, stands a carillon tower; its bells sets the tone for the campus. The tower is dedicated to my wife and me. A bronze plaque tells the story. The inscription reads in part:

To Janet Voorheis McKenna
When she enters, the room lights up;
When she leaves, everyone is singing

Whether in the grandeur of a campus carillon or the grind of a checkout counter, this is the music of her life and the message of her ministry.

29

Is a Walk
as Good as a Run?

My wife and I never fail to laugh aloud at the Aflac commercial in which Yogi Berra speaks from the barber chair, "Cash is as good as money." The barber almost drops his shears and the Aflac duck runs for cover. Yogi is the master of the malapropism.

His words came to mind when I asked myself "Is a walk as good as a run?" I had to face this question when a heart attack ended my days as a jogger and I took to walking as the alternative. I have found some comfort in the studies that show a vigorous thirty-minute walk each day is as good as a run.

But I still miss the "runner's high" that comes when the metabolism kicks into second gear. I also miss the insights that flood the mind during those exhilarating moments. So I have to count on the head-clearing and body-toning that is the result of walking.

Oh, I know all the stories of eighty-year-olds running the marathon. They are the exception. For most of us, as we age in retirement, our energy wanes and our joints get stiff. We have to be satisfied with the discipline of a long walk as our alternative to the exhilaration of more demanding exercise, such as running.

The Worth of a Walk

The apostle Paul pulls a bit of a Yogi on us when he describes the Christian life both as a run at a track meet and a walk on a path. At one minute he is comparing the Christian life to a race that requires training, discipline, perseverance, and a strong finish in order to win the prize (1 Corinthians 9:24; Galatians 5:7; Philippians 3:14; Hebrews 12:1; 2 Timothy 4:7-8). At the next minute in his letter to the Ephesians, however, he describes the Christian life as a walk (KJV), with qualities that differ from a race. Paul, urging the members of the young church to live worthy of their high calling in Christ, tells the church to walk in:

- The *humility* of Christ (4:2)
- The *image* of Christ (4:17)
- The *love* of Christ (5:1-2)
- The *light* of Christ (5:8)
- The *wisdom* of Christ (5:15)

I don't know about you, but to me, the intense competition that accompanies a race sounds a lot like the time we were in the hot pursuit of our careers. In fact, when Paul likens the Christian life to a race, he is most often referring to his own calling as an apostle or to the calling of others to the ministry of the gospel. A race is like a job. It is narrow in focus, limited in time, demanding of intense energy, involving only a segment of life, and aimed at a specific reward. Certainly, this represents Paul's view of his ministry and what our superiors expect of us when we are in career. To describe our daily work as a "rat race" may be the most accurate analogy.

When we retire, in one sense the race is over. Of course, the competition continues for our souls, but the scene changes.

A racetrack is hardly the venue for retirement. So we think instead about a long path on which we walk at a more leisurely pace. Paul's encouragement for the Ephesians to "walk" fits this picture.

Instead of picturing an athlete running on a measured track, we picture someone walking down a long path as an experience that engages the totality of our life with the totality of our world. Paul captures this thought in his letter to the Ephesians by choosing the Greek word that means "to walk around." The image of a racetrack gives way to a vision of a culture, while the snapshot of an celebrated athlete gives way to a portrait of a ordinary person.

Those of us who are retired know just what Paul means. By and large, we have run our race as great athletes and now walk a long path as everyday people. With this change, Paul's agenda for spiritual development makes perfect sense. To walk in the humility, image, love, light, and wisdom of Christ is to be worthy of his name. If we are honest with ourselves, we know that during the intensity of our working years—when we were running to keep pace with the competition—the virtues of the Christ-life were often short-changed and underdeveloped. Retirement, then, is prime time for walking, both physically and spiritually.

The Beauty of a Walk

When I was a child, a preacher gave a sermon on Enoch—the Old Testament character of whom the Scripture simply says, "Enoch walked with God, then he was no more, because God took him away" (Genesis 5:24). To illustrate this text, the preacher painted a word picture that even I could understand. He said, "One day Enoch went for a walk with God. They walked, and walked, and walked. Finally, God said, 'Enoch, we have walked until we are closer to my home than yours. Why not just come home with me?'" The picture has stayed strong in me.

Retirement is the time to take Enoch's walk. Rather than "passing away," "crossing the bar," "leaving this earth," "going to heaven," or even, "going to meet the Lord," why not envision our retirement as a time when our walk with God takes us closer to him every day? If we do so, our death will be such a natural extension of that walk that we may well hear God say, "We're closer to my home than yours. Come home with me."

30

Do You Hear
the Sound of Trumpets?

As a teenager growing up in the Big Band era, twilight time meant romance. A recent newspaper article on one of America's football greats smashes that illusion. It begins with the sentence, "At the age of seventy-five, he is in the twilight of his life."

"Wait a minute," I protested, "*I'm* seventy-five, and I reject the notion that this is my twilight." Life is too full and days are too bright to call it twilight!

So am I still entertaining the illusion that twilight means the budding of romance, not the falling shadows of death? My curiosity prompted me to read on. After completing the article, I made a list of reasons why this seventy-five-year-old football Hall of Famer was reported to be in the twilight of his life.

The Shadows of Twilight

The first and most obvious reason was that he had a rare disease that almost cost him his life. Legs that—with great speed and strength—once eluded would-be tacklers, are now permanently weakened and almost paralyzed. They remain numb. A grim prognosis puts the man in the twilight of physical life.

His spirit also seems numb. While in his prime, he was known for being thin-skinned, volatile, and profane. As he made every tackler suffer on the field, so he scorched reporters who asked "dumb" questions off the field. Still, he was admired for his candid answers and is considered an unforgettable character. But when asked about his critics in the recent newspaper article, he answered with a bleeped out word and shrugged, "I'm too old to care." It is the twilight of his spirit.

The setting for the interview with the graying star added to the twilight tone. He sits in a roomful of trophies and mementos, ever-present reminders of his glory days. Rather than bolstering his spirit, they seem to haunt him. Is he suffering from the syndrome that affects star athletes who pass their prime in their thirties and find early retirement its own form of death? The trophies themselves may cast the shadows of twilight.

Like so many successful athletes who gain fast wealth, his investments after retirement from football did not pay off. Efforts to complete his college degree failed and he turned to business ventures that only deepened his disappointment. Dregs of bitterness fill his cup when he remembers the partners and friends who idolized him on the football field, but doubted his skills in management. A routine job filled up his days until retirement. Against the brightness of memories from his football days, he would rather forget the years that followed.

So what's left? Retirement means travel, golf, and Las Vegas shows, but he has little connection with the people of his past. It's evident that twilight has surely come when a reporter asks him how to spell his name—the name that made headlines on every sports page in the nation and is permanently etched in the Pro Football Hall of Fame. It is indeed sad when the story of one's life gets summed up in these words: "As the years pile up, it seems that a world that once tried to give him everything is asking for it back, with interest."[26]

Why do I tell the story of Hugh McElhenny, better known as "the King" during his football days? Is it because I am an avid football fan and he was one of my favorites? Is it because we are the same age and I see in him my own fears? Is it because I scream in protest at the way in which the world has treated him? Or is it simply the fact that I refuse to acknowledge the twilight? Probably the answer is, "All of the above."

The Light of Dawn

There is one more question. Call it "the final question," if you will. Why did I immediately recoil at the words, "At the age of seventy-five, he is in the twilight of his life"? Every fiber in me shouted, "No, it is *not* twilight. It is the dawn!"

Here is where faith makes a huge difference. Way back in my seminary days, I read a sermon by the great Scottish preacher James Stewart, in which Stewart said,

To be redeemed is to be awakened
by the sound of a thousand trumpets
and find it bliss to be alive in such a dawn as this.

No words of human pen have inspired me more. Time and time again I have repeated them in gratitude to God. They are like a lifeline to a young man who almost drowned under repressive preaching and perpetual guilt. Better than any other words, they transformed my outlook on life from despair to hope. *This* is why my spirit rebelled when I read, "At the age of seventy-five, he is in the twilight of his life." I live in the dawn, not the twilight!

About the same time that I found such transforming power in Stewart's words, I also read J. B. Phillips's *Modern English Translation of the New Testament* and discovered these words in Romans 8:19: "The whole creation is on tiptoe to see the wonderful sight of the sons of God coming into their own."[27]

What an antidote for repressive religion or retirement blues! Time and time again I have quoted these words to uplift others and encourage myself. Best of all, neither Paul's vision nor James Stewart's celebration is age-dependent. There is nothing in the words that even hints at the idea that the dawn turns into twilight at the age of seventy-five.

If I am living in the dawn of delusion, please don't awaken me. I hear the sound of a thousand trumpets and I see all of creation standing on tiptoe as I am still coming into my own.

Oh, how I wish that my hero, Hugh McElhenny, could hear the same sound and see the same sight!

An Open Letter to Boomers and Busters

Dear Retiree-to-be:

Welcome to the unknown! You are in the bumper crop of baby boomers and busters joining your parents in retirement. You are also the first generation that feels entitled to "the good life" with the benefits of affluence.

In contrast to your parents who may have grown up in the Depression with a survival mentality and a drive to make a living, you are privileged to talk about significance and making a life. Soon, you will become the recipients of the largest transfer of wealth in human history. Thanks to our frugality, investments, and luck, if you wisely steward your inheritance, neither you nor your children will have to live on the edge of survival again.

But how will you fare when other realities of retirement hit you, especially as you grow older and have to live with the inevitability of aging? You need not be unprepared. Here are some recommendations for getting ready. They come from one who has "been there and done that."

Get Ready to Age Gracefully

Our fiftieth birthday is said to be traumatic because we suddenly realize that we have lived in the past longer than we will live in the future. Try this same thinking on for size when you approach eighty and the actuarial table gives you four-and-a-half more years.

The reminders are not subtle. I think again of the $30 check I received from the officers of my high school graduating class. Their handwritten note said: *"Due to the declining number of classmates at our 55th high school reunion, we are closing our treasury and distributing the funds equally among those of us who remain. There will be no more class reunions."* Like attendance at your own hanging, this jerk of the noose wonderfully clears the head. "We are dying" is the message. The truth came packaged in good humor, but like Macbeth's "amen," my chuckle got stuck in my throat. Wormword's old trick of making me believe that I would live forever had worked. If you think that the telltale signs of baldness, bulges, and bifocals are ominous, wait until you reach your seventies.

Get Ready to Give Yourself Away

In the midst of a career, success tends to be doing what matters to you with passion and love.[28] We set goals to be achieved, give passion to the process, and love the work we do.

Does this same definition of *success* apply to retirement? Are we still doing what matters to us—expending high energy on our passion, and loving what we do?

Sorry, baby boomers, the formula changes. If we insist on measuring success in retirement by the same definition, we will be disillusioned, disappointed, and disgruntled. Success in retirement is finding meaning in what matters to others— perhaps with less energy for passion, but with lots more love.

The maturity of this truth comes into view from personal experience. During my thirty-three years as president in high education, I had a "bully pulpit" from which to speak. Lying awake one night, I counted more than one hundred institutions of higher education where I had given major addresses—such as addresses for commencement, convocation, or lecture series. I brought with me the reputation of a person who found meaning in doing things that mattered to me, with clear-eyed passion and deep-seated love. When I retired, however, I chose writing over speaking, home over travel, and family over audiences. Of course, I lost my bully pulpit and the special sense of ministry that went with it.

What could ever replace such a powerful pulpit? Feeling guilty and empty, I asked God to give me a new ministry. He answered with a revelation while Jan and I were walking on our two-and-a-half-mile course through the lakeside village of Kirkland, Washington. Our daily walk is a circuit led by Molly, our Maltese dog, who stops at store after store to be petted and given a treat by shop-owners, receptionists, and salespersons.

Voila! My Wesleyan roots in the itinerant ministry of the circuit rider came back to me. God was using Molly to replace my bully pulpit of the presidency with a walking circuit of a common man on the street. So in the middle of the night, just as I had counted colleges where I had spoken, I counted the faces of our community friends whose story Jan and I had heard and to whom we had offered a word of hope—Jane, a beauty shop receptionist who is disillusioned with her role as a pastor's wife; Paul, a custom jeweler who lost his wife in a scuba-diving accident; Olga, an immigrant from Siberia trying to make a "go" of a lingerie shop; Judy, a salesperson of vibrant Christian faith whose dyslexia blocks her from learning computer skills; Sadie, a tattooed gardener who tends the hanging plants and flower pots along the street; Richard, a ninety-year-old man who says that he has to eat raw fish in order to drink sake; and Kyle, a bartender who shares our roots in Michigan. These people and many others are parishioners in our new congregation.

Frankly, it is more fun to anticipate our daily walks than it ever was to fly cross-country to a major speaking engagement. Success today is spelled out in terms that matter to others, reduced to a casual walk, and enriched by a deeper love.

Get Ready to Dig for Your Roots

Taunya, our property manager, combines professional toughness with delicate femininity. Every day she appears in an exquisitely matched and colorful outfit that invites a compliment. A couple of days ago, she wore a lavender pantsuit with a matching necklace of lavender balls woven on three strands. When my wife commented, "What a beautiful necklace," Taunya told the story. She said she had seen the necklace in her mind first, felt the wish to own it, and then saw it in a store window.

"If you see it in your mind first," she said, "you will have it!"

Aha, I thought, *the Law of Attraction! Taunya has been reading* The Secret, *a little neo-New Age bestseller, that promises rewards for our wishes if we just think positive.*

Sure enough, when I stopped in her office, I saw the motto of *The Secret* on the wall: "Your thoughts become things."

The spiritual search goes on. How else can we explain Rhonda Byrne's book *The Secret* selling millions of copies? Or how can we account for Rick Warren's *The Purpose Driven Life* setting records for consecutive weeks on the New York Times bestseller list? Two books could not be farther apart. One is New Age; the other is Christian. One elevates the Law of Attraction to universal truth; the other offers the love of God in Jesus Christ as our redemptive hope. Take your choice. Spiritual search is their common subject.

A wide range of options is open to you on your spiritual quest for meaning in daily life and for hope for an uncertain future. Pretenders to the throne of our soul will flash across the sky like a shower of meteorites — brilliant upon entry but ashes at the end. You will be told that you can be spiritual without God, without sacrifice, without religion, and without responsibility. Try out these theories if you wish. I only ask that you give Christian faith grounded in the Word of God and personified in Jesus Christ a chance. Like Pilgrim in *Pilgrim's Progress* or C. S. Lewis in *Surprised by Joy*, our journey may take us through a wilderness of spiritual options, but there will be signposts along the way and if we are alert, we will know when we arrive at home.

Get Ready to Finish Strong

A false notion persists about retirement as a time when life winds down and flickers out with a whimper. Age does take a toll on our bodies and sometimes on our minds, but there is no reason for our souls to shrivel and shrink. Too much is at stake. Just as you are watching members of your parents' generation to see how they age, the next generation will be watching you.

The legacy of finishing strong is an inheritance far more valuable than monetary wealth.

Don James, legendary Hall of Fame football coach, is our neighbor. He resigned as head coach of the University of Washington football team eleven days before the opening of the 1993 season because he felt he did not have the support of the University administration or the PAC-10 Conference in his contest against alleged recruiting violations. Don read my book *The Leader's Legacy*, in which I told the story of visiting "David L. McKenna Hall" on the campus of Seattle Pacific University, introducing myself to the receptionist, and having her ask, "How do you spell your last name?"

While laughing at my plight, Don added, "I know what you mean. The day after I resigned they tore down my tower!" What a cryptic account of the short-term memory of fame. A tower on the practice field symbolized the creative coaching of Don James. Rather than limiting himself to one view, or to offense, defense, or special teams, he had the perspective of the whole field from the height of his tower. No one argued with his technique when he was winning Rose Bowls and the national championship, but when he retired, his symbol went with him.

Like an old soldier, Don might have just faded away. Or he could have gone into the despair that plagues so many retired people. Fourteen years after his resignation, however, a reporter dared to ask him, "Do you regret your decision?" Rather than answering yes or no, James quipped, "I have been undefeated since 1993."

More than a good sense of humor is helping Don James finish strong. His resignation may have been controversial, but his integrity is intact. Almost every article on the glory of University of Washington football eventually cycles back to the "Don James Era."

Only with integrity can we finish strong. Erik Erikson, the psychiatrist, says that the final stage of life is a question of "integrity versus despair."[29] Integrity is holding true to your convictions and being blameless in character. Despair is having regrets unresolved and sins unforgiven. Rare is the person who can claim full integrity without a touch of despair. The rest of us can still finish strong by resolving our regrets and being forgiven for our sins. Regrets, of course, have long memories but they need not cripple us. Seen against the perspective of time, in the scope of the big picture, and within the realm of forgiveness, regrets lose their power to bedevil us. Forgiveness is the ultimate remedy for regrets and the special gift of the grace of God through Jesus Christ.

None of us need to end in despair. It is never too late to resolve our regrets and be forgiven for our sins. Think of it this way: If someone asks, "Do you have any regrets?" you can answer, "I am still undefeated!"

Yours for a strong finish,
David L. McKenna

Endnotes

1. Richard N. Ostling, "And Then There Was Billy," *Time*, November 4, 1998, www.time.com/time/magazine/article/0,9171,968894-2,00.html (accessed June 10, 2008).

2. Robert Bellah, et al., *Habits of the Heart* (Berkeley, CA: University of California Press, 2007).

3. Henri Nouwen, *In the Name of Jesus* (New York, NY: Crossroad, 1993).

4. Leo Tolstoy, *Anna Karenina* (New York, NY: Oxford University Press, 1998).

5. Kahlil Gibran, *The Prophet* (Ware, Hertfordshire: Wordsworth Editions, 1997), 7.

6. Gail Sheehy, *Predictable Crises of Adult Life* (New York, NY: P. Dutton & Company, 1976).

7. Warren Bennis and Robert Thomas, *Geeks and Geezers* (Cambridge, Harvard Business School Press, 2002).

8. Ibid.

9. Amitai Etzioni, "End Game," *The American Scholar* (spring 2005).

10. Gale Sheehy, *New Passages: Mapping Your Life Across Time*, (New York, NY: Random House, 1995), 320.

11. Lisa Birnbach, et al., *1,003 Great Things about Getting Older* (Riverside, NJ: Andrews McMeel, 1997).

12. Dave Barry, *Dave Barry Turns 50* (New York, NY: Ballantine, 1998).

13. François Fénelon, Elizabeth C. Fenn, ed., *From the Writings of Francois de Salignac de la Mothe Fenelon, Archbishop of Cambrai* (New York, NY: Morehouse-Gorham, 1952), 31.

14. Henri Nouwen, *Our Greatest Gift* (New York, NY: HarperSan-Francisco, 1994), 26.

15. Ibid, 38.

16. C. S. Lewis, *The Problem of Pain* (New York, NY: HarperCollins, 2001) chapter 9.

17. Randy L. Maddox, "Celebrating the Whole Wesley," a paper written in 2003 for the 300th anniversary of John Wesley's birth.

18. William Bridges, *The Way of Transition* (Cambridge, MA: Perseus Publishing, 2001), 72.

19. William James, *The Varieties of Religious Experience* (Cambridge, MA: Harvard University Press, 1985).

20. John R. Claypool, *Tracks of a Fellow Struggler* (London: Morehouse, 2004).

21. Justin Pope, "Surveys show young adults searching spirituality, but in new ways," *Associated Press* (April 13, 2005).

22. "Baby Boom Wealth Transfer," *Insurance Journal* (February 23, 2004).

23. John J. Havens and Paul G. Schervish, "Why the $41 Trillion Wealth Transfer Estimate Is Still Valid: A Review of Challenges and Questions," January 6, 2003, Boston College Social Welfare Research Institute, www.bc.edu/bc_org/avp/gsas/swri/swri_features_$41trillionreview.htm (accessed June 10, 2008).

24. Elisabeth Kübler-Ross, *On Death and Dying* (New York, NY: Scribner, 1997).

25. Henri Nouwen, *Here and Now: Living in the Spirit* (New York, NY: Crossroad, 2003), 19.

26. Dan Raley, "The untold story of Hugh McElhenny, the King of Montlake," *Seattle Post-Intelligencer* (September 2, 2004).

27. J. B. Phillips, trans., *The New Testament in Modern English* (New York, NY: *Macmillan*, 1958).

28. Jerry Porras, Stewart Emery, and Mark Thompson, *Success Built to Last: Creating a Life That Matters* (Upper Saddle River, NJ: Wharton School, 2007).

29. Erik H. Erikson, *Identity and the Life Cycle* (New York, NY: W. W. Norton & Company, 1980).

Printed in the United States
126966LV00001B/4/P

9 781594 980145